A Twentieth-Century American—1923–2000

Andrew F. Jannett, M.D.

VANTAGE PRESS
New York

To our Armed Forces

FIRST EDITION

All rights reserved, including the right of
reproduction in whole or in part in any form.

Copyright © 2003 by Andrew F. Jannett, M.D.

Published by Vantage Press, Inc.
516 West 34th Street, New York, New York 10001

Manufactured in the United States of America
ISBN: 0-533-14254-7

Library of Congress Catalog Card No.: 2002090357

0 9 8 7 6 5 4 3 2 1

Contents

1. Birth, Ancestry ... 1
2. Early Twentieth Century ... 18
3. School Days—Family Life ... 28
4. Naval Experience ... 44
5. Medical Education ... 64
6. Private Practice Years ... 90
7. Pony Express Physician ... 118
8. Medical Consultant, New Jersey Medicaid Program (July 1977–Sepember 1983) ... 131
9. Caretaker (September 1983–1990) ... 137
10. Marriage and Family ... 143
11. European Ancestry ... 152
12. The First Three Generations in America ... 161

Epilogue ... 167

1
Birth, Ancestry

E Pluribus, Unum

I was born on August 22, 1923, at 2:30 P.M. in the Esposito Home and Emergency Hospital in Hammonton, New Jersey. I weighed eight pounds at birth and was a normal, healthy boy.

The Esposito home belonged to Dr. Anthony L. Esposito. It was a large old mansion, which had belonged to Judge Byrnes, one of the founders of our town. Dr. Esposito, affectionately known as "Doc Spotty," bought the house a few years before my birth, and he and his wife, Myrtte, a nurse, specialized in obstetrics. The overall prenatal care, delivery, and complete care for a week or more after the birth cost seventy-five dollars.

Hammonton, New Jersey, lies in the south central part of the state and was founded sometime after the Civil War. Its flat-surfaced sandy soil lent itself to the successful growing of almost every berry, fruit, and vegetable. In size the town at my birth numbered about five thousand people.

A few weeks after my birth, I was baptized in the Roman Catholic Church by Father Sorgi of St. Joseph's Church on North Third Street in Hammonton. At the time of my baptism, Father Sorgi remarked that my hands were those of a doctor—by which he foretold my future vocation of physician and surgeon. My baptismal name was Andrew Floyd Jannett. I was named after my paternal grandfather.

My father, Albert Michael Jannett, was a healthy, robust, twenty-seven-year-old stonemason, nearly six feet tall. My mother, Margaret Mary Jannett (née Loughman), was an eighteen-year-old girl, and I was her first child. She was five feet, five inches tall and had long chestnut brown hair. My father was a first-generation Italian-American, and my mother was a first-generation Irish-American. I was a product of the Great American "Melting Pot."

Paternal Ancestry

My grandfather Fiore Andrea Giovannitti came to America from Gildone, Italy, at age nineteen and went at first to Cleveland, Ohio, to stay with relatives. In Cleveland, he met his girlfriend Emilia DiBiazio, from Gildone, Italy, and married her in the year 1893. They had their first child in the year 1894 and named her Anna. The family moved to Germantown, Pennsylvania, and my father became their second-born the following year, in December 1895. My grandparents opened a store in Germantown selling general groceries, fruit, and vegetables, and an Italian meat market. Grandfather changed his name legally in the year 1900 to Andrew F. Jannett and went into the masonry contracting business. He leased stone quarries and brought young men to work in them; the young men boarded at Grandfather's home.

In 1907, my paternal grandparents moved to Hammonton, New Jersey, with their seven children and their furniture on two large horse-drawn wagons. The main highways were gravel roads at that time.

Many Italian immigrants had settled in the Hammonton area starting about 1886. Most of the people came from Sicily, but a few of the families came from other areas of Southern Italy. My family came from Abruzzi.

My grandfather founded a masonry supply business, the Hammonton Lime and Cement Company, at 24 Front Street in Hammonton. He also went into the masonry contracting business and later purchased equipment for a house raising and moving business. He had purchased the equipment from a man named Mr. Burgess, who was retiring.

My father's siblings soon numbered seven brothers and two sisters. During the decade after arriving in Hammonton, the boys left school at an early age and worked in the business as soon as they were able. My aunts, Anna and Phyllis, worked in a nearby shoe factory operated by Mrs. Osgood and Mr. Caligne.

In 1917, my father volunteered to serve in France with the U.S. Army Ambulance Corps. Upon arrival in France, his unit was assigned to the Sixty-eighth French Army

Division (aka Blue Devils Division). His unit carried 14,000 wounded men of all nationalities to field hospitals and to some of the great cathedrals that had been converted into hospitals. After serving at the front for several months, he was granted a furlough and visited his relatives in Gildone, Italy. His grandfather was a stonemason and was busy building a church in the village. My father's mother's family ran a bakery.

After World War I, my father returned to work for his father. On November 11, 1922, my parents were married in St. Joseph Church, Hammonton. After a short honeymoon to Atlantic City, New Jersey, my parents settled in a very old two-story house with stables attached on several acres of land on Egg Harbor Road in Hammonton. My seventeen-year-old mother cried when she saw the house, and my father assured her that he would make it more livable. In addition to the aforementioned property my father purchased a new one-ton flat-bodied Model T Ford truck, and he went into business for himself as a masonry contractor. Over the ensuing forty-five years of his married life he built three new homes, with each new home built to accommodate his enlarging family. Also, he managed to send his four children through college.

Maternal Ancestry

My mother's father, Michael Loughman (pronounced "luke-mon"), came to America at age twenty in the year 1890. His father, William (Tell) Loughman, operated a dairy farm in the Golden Valley between Cork and Dublin in Ireland. My grandfather met and married an Irish immigrant girl, Julia Harrington, in Utah in 1893. She haled from the village of Eyries in county Clare in Ireland.

The young couple moved to Aspen, Colorado, a booming silver mining town, in 1893. The following year, on October 27, they had their first child, Mary Elizabeth—a redhead. Grandfather Loughman worked in the silver mines at first and later started a bottling works for whiskey. Aspen had forty saloons operating full-time in those days. Grandfather Loughman neither smoked nor drank spirits. He was also an agent for Coors Beer on the eastern slope of the Rockies.

About 1910, the silver mines filled with water, which made profitable mining impossible. Aspen became one of many ghost towns of the old West. (In 1936 or thereabouts it became a ski resort.)

Grandmother Loughman (née Harrington) was suffering from tuberculosis of the bone on one of her legs. She had a cousin who was a physician in Elizabeth, New Jersey. The family, consisting of Michael, Julia, and six of their seven children, took the long train ride from Colorado to New Jersey. The youngest child, only about one year old, was judged too young to endure the long trip. Later she joined her brothers and sister in the East. Shortly after the family's arrival in the East, Grandmother Julia Harrington Loughman was placed in a tuberculosis sanitarium. She died quietly in 1915 while still hospitalized. She was only forty-two years old. The children were placed in a Catholic orphanage in Newark, New Jersey, where they were cared for and taught by a group of German nuns. Grandfather Loughman went to Montana to aid his younger brother, who was ill.

The Loughman children were released from the orphanage as they reached an age to be gainfully employed. The oldest girl, Mary, became a telephone operator and later married Edward Feser, who was an electrician and auto mechanic.

William Loughman, the oldest boy, was placed on a chicken farm in Passaic, New Jersey, at age thirteen, and at age sixteen he enlisted in the U.S. Navy. His first ship was the USS *Yankton*, a sailing vessel.

Bernard Loughman, the second oldest, was a tailor's apprentice in Philadelphia at age fifteen, working for Browning King. In 1917 Bernard joined the U.S. Navy and was sent to the University of Pennsylvania for officers training. He was commissioned an ensign in 1918 and remained in the navy until 1923, when he retired on disability due to pulmonary tuberculosis. He was sent to Fitzsimmons Hospital in Colorado. He passed his high school and college equivalency tests and was accepted at the University of Colorado Law School. After graduation, he settled in Ventura, California, and successfully practiced law until he died in 1984 of metastatic prostate cancer. He was handsome, six feet, two inches tall, with dark curly red hair, bright blue eyes, and a ready smile. Slim and an excellent dancer, he was very bright, having skipped two grades at one time in grammar school. At eighteen years old he was the youngest commissioned naval officer during World War I in the U.S. Navy.

Lawrence H. Loughman, the third eldest of the Loughman children, was born in 1902. He was my mother's (Margaret's) favorite brother. Very bright in school, he was fair-complected, with curly blond hair, sparkling blue eyes, and a ready smile. He became a six-footer and was slim; he loved sports—especially basketball. At age seventeen he joined the U.S. Navy and was in the Medics. His older brother William, now a chief petty officer, was afraid Lawrence would be near opiates and experiment with them. William advised my Uncle Larry to get into the Deck Force and prepare for the entrance exam to the U.S. Naval Academy. One day a torpedo slipped off its rack and broke Larry's back. He spent a year in the U.S. Navy hospital in San Diego, California. Miraculously, with a deformed spinal column, he learned to walk again with only a slight limp. He came out of the navy and graduated from Drexel University in Philadelphia, Pennsylvania, as a civil engineer. He was employed by Stone and Webster Construction Company, who at the time were building the Delaware River Bridge (now the Benjamin Franklin Bridge). Uncle Lawrence found climbing too difficult and decided on law as a career. He enrolled at the University of Colorado Law School and joined his brother Bernard upon graduation in a law practice in Ventura, California. Lawrence raised five sons and died at age seventy from metastatic prostate cancer.

My mother was a twin. She was five feet, five inches tall, with chestnut brown hair and bright blue eyes, slim, and light-complected. She had a beautiful smile with straight white teeth. She had freckles on her face and arms. Her twin brother, Florie, was tall and slim, with reddish hair and freckles, and had a quiet disposition.

The youngest Loughman child was a girl, Louise, who grew up in Colorado. When she came east she lived at my mother's home for some months. Louise had auburn hair and blue eyes; she was tall with a slender build. She stuttered badly and had to whistle to enable her to catch her trend of thought and speak.

Family Anecdotes

My grandfather Andrew was a lively young man in his town of Gildone, Italy. He and his young friends played cards in the cemetery. They used an overturned tombstone for a card table. He must have been overly amorous toward Grandmother-to-be Emilia. Her uncles and brothers held Andrew on a kitchen table and threatened to "spay" him. She placed a gun in his hand and he fired blindly. One of the uncles was wounded in the neck—but only superficially. Soon after this event, Grandfather Andrew immigrated to America—in 1890. In 1893, he married Emilia in Cleveland, Ohio. They moved to Germantown, Pennsylvania, and their first child, Anna, was born in May 1894.

My grandfather Michael Loughman was brought up on a 170-acre dairy farm in Ireland. His father, William (Tell) Loughman, was an outspoken man who even told off the parish priest. He was then called "William Tell"

Loughman. He raised some horses and loved one horse in particular. One day, my grandfather Michael rode the prized horse at breakneck speed and the horse dropped dead. My great-grandmother, knowing her husband's violent temper, feared for her son's life and gave him the money to go to America. He went to the state of Utah and met Julia Harrington, an Irish immigrant girl, and they married in 1893. They moved to Aspen, Colorado, and their first child was born in October 1894.

My Italian grandparents opened a fruit, vegetable, and meat market in Germantown, Pennsylvania. My grandfather drove a horse and wagon to Dock Street in Philadelphia to buy the fruits and vegetables, while my father, Albert, slept in the straw to watch when they arrived and my grandfather made his transactions to see that no one stole their purchases. My father was big for his age and at nine his working papers were issued saying he was eleven. Eleven years was the youngest age a child could work. My father and his sister Anna, age eleven, were sent to work in Dobbins Mills from early morning until night; they set the bobbins of thread on the knitting machines. The children called the bobbins dollies. They had to stand on boxes to reach the machines. Although formal education ceased for the children, my grandfather loved music and sent my father to "Il Professore" to learn to play the cornet. At age nine my father played the cornet and my grandfather played the tuba in an Italian band. The band played in religious processions and amusement parks in the summertime.

My aunt Mary Loughman came home from St. Mary's Catholic School across from the county courthouse in Aspen, Colorado, one day in 1901 and announced that Pres. William McKinley had been shot and killed by an assassin. My grandmother Julia walked across the kitchen to the sink and put her apron to her face and began to weep.

Aunt Mary admired the family doctor, Dr. Twining, who had a beautiful house and whose eyeglasses gave him the appearance of erudition. My aunt began to complain of visual difficulties because she wanted a pair of eyeglasses just like Dr. Twining. She got the eyeglasses. However, when the children at school called her Four Eyes, her visual impairment disappeared and she never wore eyeglasses again until middle age.

My uncle Bill Loughman was two years younger than my Aunt Mary and was quite mischievous. When his sister's birthday approached he took ten dollars from his father's wallet and bought a ring for her. Bill placed it in a mound of earth, and on the way home from school with her he kicked the mound of earth. He exclaimed, "Oh, Mary, look what I found—a ring! You can have it for your birthday." When Grandfather discovered the theft of his money, he found out Bill had taken it to buy Mary a gift and he allowed Mary to keep the ring.

The Loughman family in Aspen had a horse named Rodney. He was a high-strung animal and would become quite restless when standing still in harness. My grandmother Julia, who had a way with horses, would get down from the carriage and let the horse nuzzle on her shoulder. He would become calm almost at once. My father, Albert, loved horses and from early boyhood was in charge of the Jannett family horses. He loved to curry and clean Rodney with a currycomb. Albert's father warned him against overfeeding the horse, but my father always gave the horse extra ears of corn and helpings of oats. Over the winter months, my grandfather's building business was slack and the idle horse became fat. When spring came, the horse was harnessed to a heavy-laden wagon and he would not pull. My father's younger brother Ernest built a fire under the horse to get it to move; then the horse moved forward just enough to put the wagon over the fire. Buckets of water squelched the impending conflagration.

Some Family Traits

Both the Jannett and Loughman grandparents came to the new country, America, with the work ethic and embued their children with that principle. My mother asked my father one day when I was a small boy, "I wonder what my son will be when he grows up?" My father answered, "I don't care what he'll be as long as he won't be lazy." Both families were very patriotic and loved and appreciated the opportunities available in America. Both of my grandfathers sought and obtained citizenship papers. My father volunteered for service in the U.S. Ambulance Corps in France during World War I. Also, three of my mother's brothers served in the U.S. Navy at that time. I myself served in the U.S. Navy during World War II and received three Battle Stars on the Asiatic Pacific ribbon and on the Philippine Liberation ribbon. My brother served in the U.S. Army for two years.

Finally, both families taught their children to love God and their neighbors as themselves. My father's favorite adage was "Live and let live." Also, he was proud of his work on the battlefields of France as a noncombatant and helping to save lives of members of all the nationalities engaged in the war.

Albert Jannett and Margaret Loughman on their wedding day, November 11, 1922.

2
Early Twentieth Century

O Tempora, O Mores

—Cicero

My earliest memories of growing up in Hammonton, New Jersey, were that our house was on a corner and adjacent to the Pennsylvania Railroad tracks. The property ran several hundred feet along the secondary gravel road called Line Street. During my early childhood, only the main roads were paved. All secondary roads were covered with orange-colored gravel.

Although we were only three blocks from the main street (Bellevue Avenue), we were at the end of the line for town water and sewer. Most outlying homes had outhouses or "chick sales" and pump water. In 1923, the year I was born, Hammonton, my hometown, was truly rural, with a population of slightly more than 5,000 people. The town was halfway between Camden and Atlantic City.

The distance to either large city was thirty miles, Many homes were still not wired for electricity, and local stores sold coal oil for lamps, cooking stoves, and small heaters. For the first ten years of my life we had an icebox to keep food cold in the summer. We had to remember to empty the bowl under it as the ice melted in the compartment at the top; otherwise water ran all over the kitchen floor. A card was so placed in the kitchen window to let the iceman see what size piece of ice we needed.

Our house had a pipeless heater that burned wood and/or coal. In the winter we tried not to let the fire burn out during the night by cranking the ashes, adding coal, and reducing the draft under the fire. To reduce the draft under the fire we had to leave the bottom door under the heater only slightly open. On Saturdays when I was ten years old or so I had to haul the ashes out of the cellar and crank them through a sieve to salvage pieces of coal that had not completely burned. I would then return it to the coal bin to be used again.

Although Marconi had sent a wireless message nine miles across the Salisbury

Plains of England in 1909, we did not have a radio in our home until 1930. The radio was an Atwater Kent. After one pushed the **ON** button it was necessary to wait a few minutes until the radio warmed up. Then one would turn the dial in the center to the station number desired. During my childhood, we listened to WOR from Newark, New Jersey, or WJZ from New York City. Great favorites were Lowel Thomas with the news at 6:45 **P.M.** and directly afterward *Amos & Andy*.

Henry Ford introduced the Model T Ford to America in 1908. But many farmers still brought their produce to the farmers' auction block with a horse and wagon.

Many families had gardens behind their homes with commonly used vegetables, especially Romaine lettuce and tomatoes. Some families also raised chickens and had their own fresh eggs. My grandmother Emilia Jannett had both a garden and her own chickens.

My grandfather Andrew Jannett bought grapes from California, and the family made their own wine. They made several barrels each year, which were stored in a cool cellar.

Near her garden my grandmother Emilia

had a large gazebo or "summer house." Under large shade trees, it was where she would shuck peas and prepare other vegetables for the evening meals. When winter approached many families purchased a "porker," then made their own sausage and hams and rendered their own lard.

One of my earliest memories was my parents' driving past St. Joseph Grammar School in their Model T Ford. It was 1927; the school had been started in Hammonton by the Maestre Lucia Filippine Order of nuns in 1921. My mother told me, "That is where you are going to school next year." I didn't quite know what school meant then, but ended up spending more than twenty-five years in schooling to become a physician and surgeon.

In 1927, the fourth of April to be exact, my mother went into labor. It was in the morning, and my father was already at work in Germania, New Jersey, about ten miles away from home. Mother had a dear neighbor, Mrs. Johnston, and took me across the street and asked her to care for me until my father came home from work. Mrs. Johnston called a jitney and her daughter, Lila, and they came with us to the Esposito Home. I insisted on riding with my mother and Lila Johnston in an open touring car in a driving rainstorm. My sister, Peggy, was a healthy seven-pound newborn.

In October 1927 my grandmother Emilia Jannett died at home with cancer of the liver. She was only fifty-two years old. She was seated in a large upright cushioned chair near a dining room window gasping for breath. The family doctor, A. L. Esposito, M.D., was called, and after examining her heart and lungs he shook his head to signal that the end was near. I really loved her; she always wanted to pinch my cheeks and feed me when my father brought me to visit her. I learned later in life that she had always been a very generous person to friends and neighbors, giving food and whatever else she had to share, especially to one young man who had lost his mother at age thirteen.

Upon my grandmother's death, my grandfather asked my father and mother, my sister, and myself to move into the big house and my parents to run and manage it. My father's two younger brothers, Andrew and Arthur, were still at home; they were in their midteens. In December 1927, my grandfather crossed the Atlantic and returned to his hometown of Gildone, Italy, to visit relatives and perhaps to find another wife. However, he returned to New York alone sometime after Christmas 1927. My parents hurried and took down all the Christmas decorations, as my grandfather did not appreciate such foolishness.

In 1928, my grandfather courted a schoolteacher fourteen years younger then himself. He and Cecilia Coast were married in June 1928 at St. Joseph Church in Hammonton. Cecilia was in the church choir and also played the organ there. Her first pregnancy resulted in the birth of a boy, christened Raphael George. He was Mongoloid (Down's syndrome) and died at age eight years of pneumonia. My second grandmother died of eclampsia in 1932. She refused to have a therapeutic abortion because of religious principles.

During the time my parents cared for Grandfather's home, our home was remodeled. It was reduced from a two-story house to a bungalow. It was raised and moved and a new cellar made. A front and a back porch were added. A hot water heater allowed for more frequent bathing during winter months. Prior to this invention, the water for the "Saturday Night Bath" had to be heated on the stove in large pots.

In May of 1927, Charles A. Lindbergh made the first flight across the Atlantic Ocean in his single-engine monoplane, the *Spirit of St. Louis.* The country went wild over "Lucky Lindy." Songs were written about him, tickertape parades were held, and even children's clothes were made to honor the famous flyer. My new grandmother bought me a brown raincoat complete with aviator's helmet and goggles. I was so proud to wear it I couldn't wait until it rained.

Soon my new grandmother, Cecilia, assumed the burdens of running the big house and rearing my father's two younger brothers, Andrew and Arthur. The new arrangement didn't last long. When the two boys would be seated for mealtime, the veteran "schoolmarm" would ask them to spell certain words, such as *spaghetti.* My Uncle Andy said, "Hell, I didn't want to spell spaghetti; I wanted to eat some." The two boys went to live with their oldest sister, Anna, and went to work in Aunt Anna's husband's bakery. My parents, together with my baby sister and myself, returned to live in our remodeled home at 318 South Egg Harbor Road in Hammonton.

A "party line" telephone was installed and our number was 449-*J. This line had several people on it and allowed many an old gossip to have entertainment. In our newly remodeled home, we had a new gas stove, complete with a coin meter in the basement. Before supper, my mother would insert a quarter in the meter to turn the gas on for cooking. Our first gramophone was replaced by a wind-up RCA Victrola. The turntable was on the top, and a compartment to hold records was on the bottom. A "well" for new needles was on top of the turntable. Popular songs in my early childhood were "Yes, We Have No Bananas," "Barney Google," "The Sheik of Araby," "Baby Face," and a little later a tearjerker with Al Jolson, "Sonny Boy."

Popular sports figures in those days were Jack Dempsey and Babe Ruth. My father had borrowed a battery radio to hear the Dempsey-Tunney rematch. The radio failed to function in the fourth round, and my father went to a nearby "lunch car" run by Sam

Abba. My mother predicted Tunney's victory in the first and second bouts.

The first movies that I saw were silent films, and even though I could not read the captions I enjoyed the action on the screen and the piano music. One night, my Uncle Andy was "slap shining" his shoes and dressed in his best suit. I inquired, "Where are you going, Uncle Andy?"

"I am going to the Rivoli Theater to see a movie called *The Jazz Singer* with Al Jolson; it is a talkie." I asked if I could go with him; he replied a big, "No."

My favorite thing as a child was penny candy. Without my mother's knowledge I grubbed pennies from my Grandfather Jannett: "Do you have any pennies, Grandpop?" With ceremony he put his left hand in his pocket and brought out a handful of change. I waited expectantly while he sorted out five or six pennies. I would go immediately to the candy store run by John Jacobs on Twelfth Street in Hammonton. My favorite purchase was two Mary Janes or Tootsie Rolls for one penny. Five cents bought a nice treat.

Mother did the laundry in a large tub with

a scrubbing board. When she did my younger sister's diapers Mother called it doing "my daily dozen." She loved to put her laundry out in the air to dry on the line. In winter, the clothes froze. She ironed all articles, shirts, sheets, pillowcases, handkerchiefs, etc. Although she did not have a washing machine at that time, she did have a large Singer sewing machine complete with foot treadle and bobbins of different-colored thread and spare needles. She even made a suit for me to go to school when I was five years old. It was cut out of one of my father's blue serge suits: short pants with shoulder straps. She made a rounded-collar pongee blouse with large white buttons; a large dark blue bow tie, white ribbed high stockings, and patent-leather shoes completed the ensemble.

She had cut my hair with bangs, and the reaction of the boys from the farms at my appearance was not good. I will describe it in chapter 3: "School Days—Family Life."

3
School Days—Family Life

Ad Astra

Grade One

Although, I had just had my fifth birthday on August 22, 1928, my mother asked Sr. Anna Furia, the Mother Superior of the Maestre Lucia Filippine order, to allow me to start first grade. The school was St. Joseph Roman Catholic School, founded in Hammonton in 1921. Mother told the nun that I had no little friends at home and even if I couldn't do the work, I was young enough to repeat the year.

    I lived eight blocks from the school, and so the first few days Mother accompanied me to the school. The first-grade teacher was a very thin young girl with rosy red cheeks; she seemed almost overwhelmed with the large number of youngsters in her class.

    As soon as my mother left, I announced

to Sister Stella, the first-grade teacher, that I was going home. I headed for the door. She blocked my exit and returned me to my seat. Later when I thought she wasn't looking, I climbed up on a radiator nearby and prepared to jump out the window. It was a considerable distance. Fortunately, she caught me and in desperation gave me a resounding slap on the face. This was my first experience with discipline outside my home.

Later that day, a group of boys surrounded me in the schoolyard at recess and just gawked at my homemade suit, pongee blouse, white ribbed stockings, and patent-leather shoes. One of them decided he didn't like what he saw and pushed me into a mud puddle.

I soon became adjusted to school and my first-grade reader, complete with pictures. I liked reading but found arithmetic a real puzzle until my mother used stick matches on the dining room table to demonstrate addition and subtraction. The sentences in the first-grade reader included "The hen is in the box" and "The egg is in the hay." I liked them because of how the pictures fit the reading lesson, and Sister Stella turned our to be a good teacher. I was doing well in first grade until I became ill with a very sore throat and a high fever and then a rash. The family doctor, Dr. A. L. Esposito, diagnosed scarlet fever, and my home was quarantined. My sister, Peggy, went to live at my Uncle Andy and Aunt Pearl's house. The doctor came daily to visit me for a week or two. His fee was one dollar for a house call and fifty cents for an office visit. Finally, I shed all my skin as the exanthema of the disease cleared. Our house was fumigated by Dr. Charles Cunningham; we had to remain away from the home for an afternoon. When my mother and I returned home we had to throw all the windows open to get rid of the horrible odor.

On Election Day in November 1928, my mother took me to the Myers store polling booth on South Egg Harbor Road in Hammonton. The former governor of New York, Alfred E. Smith, was running against Herbert C. Hoover for president of the United States. My mother was a Democrat. My father was a Republican but changed after Hoover's term (1929–1933). When my mother left the polling booth, an elderly woman, Mary O————, was near the doorway. She blurted out, "I guess we know who that Irish papist voted for!"

As we passed by, I asked, "What is an Irish papist?"

My mother said, after we were out of earshot, "Don't pay any attention to her; she's drunk."

The country wasn't ready for a Catholic president, and Herbert Hoover won. Meanwhile, I became more adapted to school and the nun's discipline. There were about twenty five little classmates, roughly one-half boys and one-half girls. The boys' benches were on one side of the room and the girls' were on the other. Blackboards were in the front of the classroom, and over them were plaque cards with ABCs—capital and small letters—and the numbers. Above all and in the center was a picture of George Washington, with an American flag on each side. We said the Pledge of Allegiance and a short prayer before starting classes.

The first class every day was Religion and the recitation of the catechism. I still remember the first questions and answers: "Who made the world? God made the world. Where is God? God is everywhere. Why did God make you? He made me to love him in this world and forever in the next." One of my best friends was a boy about a year older named Joseph Baker. Joe and I walked back and forth to school each day together.

My father's business prospered. He was a masonry contractor. He belonged to the American Legion and the Veterans of Foreign Wars. My father's friends called him Ollie for Al. He was popular and was known as one of the boys who fought at the front in World War I. Also, he was a skilled bricklayer and stonemason and was a fast worker who did reasonably priced houses. He was always kept busy in his own hometown and had a regularly paced life. Breakfast was at seven in the morning, lunch at twelve noon, and supper at 5:30 P.M. The family always sat around the table for meals, and "children were to be seen and not heard." At the evening meal, my mother would say, "Be quiet; your father has had a hard day at work."

At the end of my first year in school, my mother was pleased to inform me that I had passed to the second grade. Summers were always a thrill and a joy after the long school year. We played games of all types, hide and seek, marbles, etcetera. It seemed that the Lord had not put enough hours in a day. Our favorite memory was of Mr. Venuti and his very colorful ice-cream wagon pulled by a single horse. A large ice-cream cone could be had for five cents. He would fill a large plate for a quarter. Hucksters of all types were common then. Mr. Rufus Seely had a pushcart with vegetables. Mr. Leonard had an ancient truck from which he sold cakes and pies. Mr. Basile sold fish from a huckster truck. He weighed the fish, cleaned them on the spot, and wrapped the purchases in newspaper.

In the second grade my teacher was Sister Rita. She was short, somewhat stout, and red-faced. She was very kind to me. One day I told her that my mother would not give me a second bowl of lima bean soup. Sister Rita took me by the hand to the convent kitchen, sat me down, and made me a large banana sandwich using two thick pieces of Italian bread. I didn't think I could eat it all, but somehow I managed to get it all down.

I made my First Communion that year as I reached the "Age of Reason." The great Stock Market Crash occurred in the month of October of 1929. But for most of the families in our town we had no notion that it would be the prelude to ten years of economic depression. At the end of my second year in school, my friend Joe Baker and I were given medals at the Commencement Exercises as the two best pupils. We repeated in the fourth, fifth, sixth, and eighth grades.

The economic depression hit every family hard in 1931, 1932, and 1933. A truckload of produce was bought in the city and sold for less than ten dollars. My father's work slacked off, but yet he managed to keep busy working for schoolteachers, police officers, and government workers, who had the good jobs.

On December 11, 1931, my brother, Albert Michael Jannett, was born. He was a full-term baby and weighed eight pounds at birth.

I was now in the third grade and began to learn the multiplication tables, under Sister Anna. She was very quiet but did a good job teaching us. During the winter months of 1932, I contracted whooping cough and was quite ill for a few weeks.

I caught up with my work and passed to fourth grade. We began to learn fractions. I remember my mother sitting down with me at the dining room table and cutting an apple with a knife to demonstrate halves, quarters, and eighths.

I took piano lessons from Miss Anna E. Bowker on South Egg Harbor Road in Hammonton, opposite the train station. A one-hour lesson was fifty cents. I went each Saturday at ten in the morning. She had a large green parrot in a cage in her sun parlor. When I rang the bell the parrot called out, "Anna, someone is at the door!" and repeated the announcement several times. Miss Bowker used the John Williams method of graded pieces of music for their difficulty. Later my two sisters and brother also took lessons from her. My mother skimped on her "bean money" to pay for the lessons. Later my sisters took dancing lessons and monologue lessons. Since it was a depression era my father complained that there were "too many leaks." Dad economized by stopping smoking Camel cigarettes. He switched to a pipe and Prince Albert pipe tobacco in a red can. My father also began to cut my hair to save money. He had hand clippers, a barber comb, and scissors. Also, he bought a shoemaker's outfit to put on new heels, rubber soles, and metallic taps. We frequently wore out the tips of our soles; he put taps there.

One day, when I was eight or nine years old, I found a five-dollar bill along a curb in front of the American Store on Main Street. I was collecting bottle caps from soda bottles and match covers. This hobby led to this discovery of the five-dollar note. I went home and got my express wagon with sides on it and went to the American Store, where the manager, David Longo, knew me because I shopped there for my mother. I proceeded to buy all the different fruits and vegetables that I liked. Large numbers of oranges, grapefruits and bananas were piled into my wagon. I spent four dollars and eighty-six cents. I could hardly pull my wagon home. When my mother saw my purchases, she said, "Did you steal them?"

"No," I replied. "I found five dollars."

Then she said mournfully, "Some poor soul must have lost the money." Nonetheless, we all enjoyed the windfall.

Sometime in 1932, our family doctor, A. L. Esposito, referred my mother to a specialist in Philadelphia at the Hahnemann

Hospital. The diagnosis was chronic appendicitis. My mother asked the specialist how much the operation would cost. He replied, "Three hundred dollars." My mother said her appendix would have to remain in her if it cost that much to remove it. For $150 she had the operation, and she recovered uneventfully.

My father sold one-half of our property on Egg Harbor Road to the Gulf Oil Company for fifteen hundred dollars. The oil company built storage facilities and a gasoline station. We still had an extensive side yard where we later built a new home.

The year 1933 was a milestone; Franklin Delano Roosevelt was elected president of the United States. Although the deep depression continued, a wave of optimism overtook Americans. Prohibition was repealed. A song of the day was "Happy Days Are Here Again."

The new administration was called the New Deal and promised to help the "forgotten man." Once again there was talk of a bonus to be given to veterans of World War I. This became a reality for my father in 1936. He received $1,500.

My mother figured all my father's work.

She always said, "I could not make a mistake because I knew how hard he worked."

My father was awarded the contract to build Olivo's Market on Central Avenue in 1933. The masonry work included doing all the footings, pouring a concrete foundation, laying nearly 100,000 bricks, and doing all the lathing and plaster, sidewalks, etcetera, for the sum of $3,300. The owner, Rocco Olivo, bought all the material.

My mother's figuring came within a few hundred bricks on that contract. She was always very accurate with her mathematics.

Our neighborhood consisted of many ethnic and religious groups. We called ourselves the Cherry Street Gang. The children were Catholic, Protestant, and Jewish. They were Italian, Irish, German, English and occasionally black. As a child, I never heard any disparaging remarks over race, creed, or nationality. My father always said, "Live and let live."

As children, we all had roller skates and homemade scooters and some of us had bicycles. I had a red two-wheeler with a siren. The boys in those days called it a sy-reen.

We children always had a dog. My first

dog's name was Spot. My grandfather's Airedale was Jack. In the middle of grammar school days, my dog was a beautiful brown dog, Brownie, who followed me to school each day and was waiting outside to walk home with me at three o'clock. This animal was hit by a car and died and was replaced by another dog, a black-and-white one that I called Pal. When I was about twelve years old, my dog Pal got into a fight with a vicious German shepherd. The undersurface of Pal's neck was badly wounded, with a long, jagged laceration. I washed and cleaned the wound with soap and water. Then I shaved all the hair. Pal lay still without a whimper while I sewed the edges of the wound together with a straight needle and black thread from my mother's sewing box. Then I smeared a yellow "healing salve" on and made a bandage. Several days later when I took the stitches out, there was a clean light pink scar line. I was thrilled with the results. My later life as a surgeon—when I took care of sick human beings—gave me no more satisfaction than I had when I cared for my dog.

In June 1936, I graduated from grammar school. I received a one-ounce gold medal. It was the English Award and my name and the date and ST. JOSEPH'S GRAMMAR SCHOOL was engraved on it.

My mother had planned for me to go to a Catholic high school. An answer to her prayer was the founding of St. Joseph's High School in 1935. The Pallottine Fathers sent five young boys to study there under the direction of Fr. Lucien Abbate, our pastor, and the good Maestre Filippine nuns, Mother Superior Mary DeCarlo and her assistants Sisters Gilda and Antoinette Dal Corso, who were real-life sisters.

The first class with lay students started in September 1936. It consisted of four boys and three girls. The classes were held on the second floor of St. Joseph's School on North Third Street in Hammonton. The former gymnasium was converted into classrooms. My father had done the lathing and plastering for this project.

The high school years were happy ones. We used the old St. Joseph's Church on North Third Street for our gymnasium and the Carnival Grounds on French Street for football and baseball games. During summer months, I worked with my father in the masonry business.

On July 8, 1937, my sister Kathleen was born in the Esposito Home. It was a very hot day—more than 100 degrees Fahrenheit. After work, I cleaned up, put fresh clothes on, and went into town. I stopped in Godfrey's Drug Store on Main Street and purchased a one-pound box of Whitman's chocolates for ninety-five cents. I then visited my mother with my gift and saw my baby sister. She was the last addition to our family.

The schooling that we received in St. Joseph's High School in Hammonton was excellent. We received a thorough grounding in literature, algebra, geometry, trigonometry, and, of course, Latin. There were hours of homework and recitation and blackboard working out of problems. It was a daily mental "strip tease" before the teacher and your peers.

In my last year of high school, my mother asked me if I would like to go to college. I replied that I would be pleased to go. She had hoped that I would become a lawyer and join her two brothers in California. When I announced that I wanted to be a physician, my parents warned me that it was a very long course of study. I replied that I would study medicine or I would not go to college at all.

In September 1940, I matriculated at La Salle College, a Christian Brothers school at Twentieth Street and Olney Avenue in Philadelphia. It was a small all-boys school with a strong premed course. The Biology Department was under the direction of a proper Englishman—Dr. Roland Holroyd. His Ph.D. was obtained at the University of Pennsylvania.

There were fifty-five premed students in my class. They were mostly from Philadelphia and had attended the excellent high schools of the city—especially prominent was Central High down the block from La Salle. I was fearful of the competition. After each test, the marks were posted on "the Wailing Wall." After the first test I came out eighth and it gave me confidence that I could compete.

The years passed very swiftly. After the United States declared war on Japan, Germany, and Italy in December 1941, we were placed on an accelerated program. I graduated in September 1943 and immediately volunteered in the U.S. Navy in the V-7 officers' training program. I was twenty years old, with a B.A. degree in biology and a minor in chemistry.

4
Naval Experience

Veni, Vidi, Vici

I was called to active duty and sent to the U.S. Naval midshipman program at the University of Notre Dame in South Bend, Indiana. I had decided to put my medical training in abeyance until the war was over. The training program at Notre Dame was intense—both physically and mentally. We received training in navigation and celestial piloting, seamanship, gunnery, damage control, and communications. I graduated on May 31, 1944, with a commission in the U.S. Naval Reserve. My rank was Ensign. Eleven hundred boys started in my class and about seven hundred were successful.

    I was assigned as the fourth officer to Landing Craft Infantry 1075. The ship was in the process of being built by DeFoe Shipbuilding Company in Bay City, Michigan. This company also built larger ships such as destroyer escorts. I arrived in Bay City on a Saturday afternoon. A taxi driver asked where I wanted to go. I replied that I needed to find a place to live for one month. I checked my bags and he took me to a large home on Fourth Avenue, which had a number of naval officers living there. The proprietress told me at first that she was filled up. As I went to descend the steps, she announced that she would give me her room. The patriotic fervor of our citizenry during World War II was simply amazing. Mrs. Cora Martindale assisted me in collecting records, books, and games for my ship. She was a very good landlady.

Toward the end of June 1944, the other three officers and twenty-five-man crew arrived. The skipper was twenty-seven-year-old Raymond Smiley—trained as an accountant in civilian life. He was of medium height and fair-complected and had blue eyes and sandy hair. He was of pleasant disposition and held the rank of lieutenant (junior grade). Buck Wagner was to be the executive officer. He was more than six feet tall, broad-shouldered and beetle-browed, with a crew cut. He was a soft-spoken southerner from North

Carolina. When he spoke, the crew listened. He held the rank of ensign and was, like myself, a "ninety-day wonder," from Northwestern University Midshipman School. He was a few years older than I. Harvey Packer, age twenty-five, was the engineering officer. He also was an ensign. He had a good knowledge of the ship's engines, generators, and oil and water storage tanks. He and I shared the same cabin for about a year. A few of our crew were seasoned sailors, but most were greenhorns; they would learn on the "high seas." The boatswain was named Reed; the gunner's mate was Ivy. Kenneth Thamman was an alert eighteen-year-old signalman. Woodward was the radio operator. Henderson, a huge Swede, was the leader of the "Black Gang," or engine crew. The pharmacist's mate was Favreau—a fair-haired, gentlemanly person from Geneva, New York. "Cookie" was Richard Wood and his assistant was a stout boy named Cinquegrano from Garfield, New Jersey. The remainder of the crew were mostly deck hands—who kept our vessel clean and "shipshape." They were divided into port and starboard groups.

Finally, Captain Patch accepted the ship

Bay City, Michigan, June 1944 (left to right) Lt. Raymond Smiley (Captain) Butler, PA; Ens. Harvey Packer (Engineer) Brooklyn, NY; Ens. Andrew Jannett (4th Officer) Hammonton, NJ; Ens. "Buck" Wagner (Executive officer) Albemarle, NC; (Above) Crew of twenty-four.

into the navy and commissioning exercises were held and we moved aboard Love, Charlie, INT 1075. The ship LCI (L) 1075 was 158 feet long, with a beam of 27 feet at its widest. Its draft was shallow, 6 1/2 feet forward and 13 feet aft. It was flat-bottomed and painted dark jungle green, so we knew we were headed for the Pacific theater of war. Eight 6-71 diesel GM engines arranged into port and starboard quads powered the ship.

Each quad was harnessed to a bull gear, which in turn was fastened to a reversible-pitch electrically controlled propeller. Total power was 1,800 HP. We carried 30,000 gallons of fuel but only 14,000 gallons of water. We had no evaporators to produce water, so we later learned to shower with salt water. I was in charge of the communications and the commissary departments. We had enough dry stores to last six months but only enough fresh provisions for six weeks. We soon learned to live on powdered milk, powdered eggs, and dehydrated fruits and vegetables of every type.

After a "shakedown cruise" on Lake Huron, we sailed through the Straits of MacKinac and down Lake Michigan to Chicago. We "tied up" at Hodgkin's coal yard and awaited two truckloads of fresh foods from the Great Lakes Naval Training Center. A friend named Ensign Carol Woodruff had allowed me to get a generous supply of fruits, vegetables, eggs, ice cream, boned beef, and barrels of chickens. When the supplies arrived, I found that I did not have enough storage room in our freezer and vegetable locker. I had to store the chicken barrels under tarpaulins surrounded by ice on the fantail.

As we sailed down the Illinois River and the Mississippi River, I ordered the cook to serve chicken as often as possible and to give the crew ice cream every night until we overcame the oversupply. As we passed down the Mississippi River we stopped at Saint Louis, Memphis, Baton Rouge, and New Orleans. One of the crew reported to the captain that I allowed the crew to have ice cream in soup bowls each night when he was ashore. He called me into his cabin and wanted to know how much the daily cost was for each member of the crew. The allotment was $1.05 and I was spending a $1.50 a day. He yelled at me, "Andy, what are you trying to do, win a popularity contest?" Later, when we arrived in the war zone, each man was fed for $.45 per day!

A Commander Federson of the Coast Guard piloted our ship down the Mississippi River. The big sternwheelers the *Memphis* and the *Delta Queen* fascinated me. They conjured memories of Mark Twain and *Tom Sawyer, Huckleberry Finn,* and other pleasant childhood books. When we arrived in New Orleans, we had to replace our heat exchangers because they were fouled with mud from the river. From New Orleans we headed to Galveston, Texas. I began to stand my first night watches in the conning tower. At Galveston, we completed further training until we had an efficient and cohesive group. The night before we left the United States, the crew was given liberty ashore. Many relieved themselves of any amorous feelings at the Majestic Hotel.

Our next port of call was Colón, Panama, on the Atlantic side of the canal. It was August 22, 1944, and my twenty-first birthday. I was surprised when the skipper wished me a Happy Birthday and ordered me to go ashore and "enjoy yourself." Ashore in Colón, Panama, that evening, I happened to saunter down Cash Street. I noticed that there were many "ladies" sitting on little stools in front of their houses, and through the front windows I saw beds with brightly colored bedspreads. I thought this was indeed strange, since it was drizzling and the ladies were getting wet. When some of the ladies reached out for my hand, I decided to return to my ship. When I got back aboard, Captain Smiley said, "Andy, did you have a good time?"

"Yes," I answered.

He said, "It's only nine-thirty."

I made no reply.

We passed through the Panama Canal and the locks at night. I thought the canal was a great engineering feat. We then arrived in Panama City on the Pacific side and received further supplies before embarking on our long voyage across the Pacific Ocean.

We left Panama City on August 25, 1944, in company with four mine sweepers. Each mine sweeper in turn developed some engine problem and requested permission to go to the San Diego, California, Naval Base for repairs. Before the last of them left, I asked the skipper if we might go with them. "No," he replied. "If we lose any time, we'll miss the invasion and retaking of the Philippine Islands." So we continued on the long voyage alone. We headed southwesterly, north of Galapagos Islands, and crossed the Equator and were all duly initiated into the Royal Order of Lobsterbacks. I was the assistant navigator and had to learn a new set of constellations and navigational stars. Capt. Smiley enjoyed pointing out the constellation of the Southern Cross. I did the daily LAN sun shot that gave longitude but not latitude. The skipper always got good "cuts" on his star sights. We kept track of our course and speed with dead reckoning but corrected position with daily star sights using the sextant. We averaged ten to twelve knots, or standard speed. On September 13, we arrived at Bora Bora in the Society Islands. Tahiti is in the same group. It was a beautiful island with snow-white sand and tall palm trees surrounded by deep blue water.

I had had nearly three weeks to make up a shopping list of fresh food supplies we needed. Soon after tying up, the skipper told me to see the supply officer. Our layover would be only overnight. The supply officer roared with laughter when I read my shopping list. "Why are you laughing?" I asked.

He replied, "All the things you ask for we wish we had ourselves. Look out the window."

I saw a pile of boxes as high as a house.

He said, "Take a work party of ten or twelve men; rummage through the boxes. You may get lucky and find some canned chicken and, if you're real lucky, some canned fruit cocktail." So there would be no more boned beef, ice cream, oranges, fresh eggs, or fresh anything. I looked around the island and I saw bananas growing. I contacted a native with a large outrigger canoe. I asked him how much he wanted for a boatload of bananas. He said he wanted ten American dollars. I told him I would give him five American dollars. He agreed to bring the bananas that evening. Why not this afternoon? He said, "No have own banana plantation." That evening under bright moonlight we loaded the bananas. We hung the stalks of green bananas on wire on the well deck to be exposed and ripened in the sun. We visited the small officers' club that evening and signed the guest register. A few pages before ours, we saw that Eleanor Roosevelt, FDR's wife, had visited Bora Bora before us.

The next day, September 14, 1944, we continued our voyage westward and south of the Tonga (Friendly) and Fiji Islands. We were headed for Espiritu Santo Island in the New Hebrides Islands. During this long leg of our journey, we stood monotonous watches of four hours on duty and eight hours off. One day a whale swam parallel to our ship for a few hours. On another day a large albatross landed on our ship, regurgitated some food, and after a few hours left. We whiled away the long hours with reading and writing letters to our loved ones in hopes of mailing them someday. Members of the crew listened to the same records over and over again. I can still hear the scratchy renditions of the hand-cranked record player. "I'll Be Seeing You," "Rose of Santa Rosa, I'll Be Back Someday," and "Amore" were favorites. Scuttlebutt, or false rumors, abounded—stories about "mail buoys" in the middle of the Pacific Ocean had young sailors believing them. We had frequent fire drills, general quarters battle station drills, and abandon ship drills. I had the duty to place all secret communications in a weighted canvass bag and consign same to the "Deep Six" or "Davey Jones' Locker." Also, I had to place an explosive charge in our radio and newly invented recognition device so that it would not fall into enemy hands. Each member of the crew was assigned a task in case of abandoning ship—responsibility for releasing life rafts, filling water casks, getting food rations, signal guns, and flares, etcetera.

A severe storm occurred and lasted three days. The winds were strong and the waves washed over the conning tower. The flat-bottomed LCI bobbed like a cork on such a sea. Lifelines were rigged topside to keep men from being washed overboard. Eating anything but hand-held food was impossible. When the storm abated and we could take star sights we were 105 miles from our dead reckoning position. The set of the wind and sea accounted for the disparity. When we arrived at Espiritu Santo Island, the skipper sent me ashore in a wherry (a light rowboat). Two men rowed me ashore. As soon as they dropped me off, I felt very alone. My task was to find the naval supply depot and signal my ship as to its location. Although I had a loaded .45-caliber pistol in a side holster, I was scared. I found a pathway in a jungle setting and followed it. I soon came upon a group of very primitive natives wearing loincloths and carrying spears. I never presented my back to them as I passed warily.

After a long trek, I found the base and was never as happy as then to see fellow Americans. My ship was contacted and proceeded to the base. A cook at the base gave me some apple pies to bring back to my ship.

The next stop on our voyage was Manus Island in the Bismarck Archipelago. There was a huge armada of ships assembled at Manus. They were poised here awaiting orders for the invasion of Leyte in the Philippines on October 12, 1944. Our ship was sent to Jautefa Bay in New Guinea to join our flotilla of twenty-four LCIs and undergo further training together as a unit. We went to a beautiful island in the Helmaheras called Mios Woendi. Practice landings were performed repeatedly by each officer in turn on each ship. We had to discharge up to 250 men in four and one-half minutes.

One bright, sunny, very hot morning it was my turn to practice landings over and over for four hours—from 8:00 A.M. until 12 noon. I was exhausted and went to my cabin to rest. I was so tired that I only removed my hat and shoes before I lay on my bunk. I fell into a sound sleep. Meanwhile, my roommate, Harvey Packer, began his four-hour stint of practice landings. After only about one half hour, I awakened suddenly, sat bolt upright, and put my shoes on but did not tie the laces. I stumbled out of my cabin in a semiconscious state. I walked twenty to thirty feet down the passageway. Suddenly there was a great crashing noise and our ship lurched to starboard. An alarm sounded. Some crew members shouted, "Collision!" amid the ship's port side. I followed the damage control men and peered through the doorway of my cabin. The bow of another ship had plowed into my cabin and was stuck there. The bunk I had just left was demolished. I was determined to go to the next religious service I could find to thank God.

We were ordered to Leyte in the Philippines in December 1944. The Japanese still occupied Luzon and Manila and airfields there and on Mindanao. Several air raids were directed against us on Christmas Day. A resupply convoy was ordered to San José, Mindora, in the last week of December 1944. The convoy had to pass through the Mindanao Strait. The Japanese still had air superiority and we were subject to constant attacks, day and night. We lost several ships to kamikaze—suicide planes.

One ship, the *William Boyd*, was loaded with ammunition and high-octane gasoline. The brave men aboard the ship fired at a diving kamikaze plane until the last minute. The ship was a few hundred yards in front of us. The explosion was a gigantic red ball of fire.

The concussion in the air caved one's chest and even your eyeballs felt like they were bulging. The ship completely disappeared and a large hole in the water was to be momentarily seen. Later as we sailed on we saw torsos of men in life jackets minus heads, arms, and legs.

During one engagement, a Japanese plane tried to crash into a ship in line ahead of us. My gun crew, on starboard side, hit it down the middle with 20mm shells. Its wing hit the water, and it exploded before it could do any damage. When we reached San José, Mindoro, the Japanese air raids were frequent and intense. A destroyer was lying on its side in the harbor, and a tanker was burning. No sooner had we arrived than the supply ship, *Orestes*, was hit with a 500-pound bomb and thirteen officers were killed in the wardroom. As for myself, I slept topside with all my clothes and a life jacket on for about one week. A task force of small ships, LCIs and PT boats, made a mock invasion of Lucena, Luzon. We fired rockets and sent false messages. This operation kept three Japanese divisions in the southern part of the island.

Gen. Douglas MacArthur gave our task force a unit citation for a job well done.

On January 9, 1945, we landed troops at Lingayen Gulf, about ninety miles north of Manila. Our forces soon captured Manila and the air bases. Then our air forces assumed command of the skies. We loved to see the P-38s with their twin fuselages and rudders in aerial combat with Japanese Zero airplanes. Mopping up Japanese army units left behind on Mindoro occupied our time until March 1945, when we invaded Zamboanga, Mindanao. Four U.S. cruisers took part in the bombardment of the city. They were the *Boise, Cleveland, Montpelier,* and *Phoenix.*

In April, our flotilla returned to New Guinea to pick up Australian troops for an invasion of British northwest Borneo at Brunei Bay. At this time, we were all saddened to hear of the death of President Roosevelt. All of our ships in the Seventh Fleet flew our flags at half-mast. Before we left for Borneo, General MacArthur visited our task force. We stood at attention as he passed by in a launch. He was the commander of the Seventh Fleet. When his launch approached the gangway of our flagship, the *Blue Ridge,* he motioned with his index finger for Adm. Turner Joy to come down in his launch. MacArthur was indeed an imperious personage.

After the Brunei Bay invasion, we returned to Leyte in the Philippine Islands. In May 1945, we were overjoyed to learn of Germany's unconditional surrender. Now we began to receive mail from home on a regular basis. My mother wrote me a letter every day before she went to bed. She always managed to include some item of interest. About this time, in June or July 1945, we received the operation plan—Victoria. It was the plan for the invasion of the Japanese home islands.

In August 1945, I was called to our flagship to receive a radiogram to return to the continental limits of the United States. Just before I left Manila, aboard a large transport, the USS *Sea Partridge,* I heard of the bombing of Hiroshima and Nagasaki. No one knew exactly what an atomic bomb was. We did know that the Japanese government surrendered unconditionally and precipitously. The *Sea Partridge* was a C5 cargo ship. It was fitted out to carry 5,000 men—3,500 soldiers of the Forty-second Division and 1,500 sailors. I was appointed sanitation officer and directed a work force of forty-eight men and two chief petty officers. During our trip across the Pacific en route to Seattle, Washington, we heard of the sinking of the USS *Indianapolis* and the loss of many sailors. A Japanese submarine commander was unaware that Japan had surrendered four days before the sinking of the *Indianapolis*.

We arrived in Seattle, Washington, on a bright sunny morning. The view of Mount Rainier with its snowcapped peak was spectacular.

As ours was the first large transport to return stateside after the war, our reception both in the harbor and on shore made us proud to be American servicemen. I crossed the country by train. My parents and younger brother Albert and younger sister Kathleen were delighted to see me. My sister Peggy had enrolled in Syracuse University in New York. I visited her one weekend when Gen. Jonathon Wainwright spoke to the students. He had surrendered to the Japanese on Bataan and had been a prisoner of war. He still appeared emaciated.

The navy ordered me to gunnery school in Southern California. After one month, I was ordered back to San Pedro Bay, Philippine Islands, to take command of the USS LCI (L) 1056. I was not a little frightened, as I was only twenty-two years old. When I joined the complement of the 1056 we were sent to Subic Bay. The young skipper whom I was to replace had been on the water for twenty-seven months. He looked "burnt out." Before I assumed command, he took his ship to Manila. The next day we crossed Manila Bay and traveled between Bataan Peninsula and Corregidor and headed north to Subic Bay. The day was clear and windy. As we crossed Subic Bay, an LCM motor launch with five British sailors tried to cross in front of us. Traveling at full speed, we could not stop in time. We struck them broadside. The boat was demolished. The British sailors were sucked under by our propellers, and all perished. The young skipper of 1056 began to cry. He was scheduled to fly home the next day. I said, "I've just returned from home. We were not at fault. I'll face the music; you go home." He left the next day and I assumed command. He was most grateful and corresponded with me for many years.

    A Court of Inquiry was convened, and

several months passed before the Office of the Philippine Sea Frontier under Vice Admiral Kaufman and the British Naval Authorities rendered a verdict of no fault on my part. During the legal proceedings, my legal adviser was Lt. (j.g.) Gabriel Tucker. Two years later, I met him at the same table, same medical fraternity (Phi Chi), and same medical school—Johns Hopkins. We were in the same class at medical school.

In August 1946, I returned stateside on a slow transport—the *General Grant.* We passed through the Panama Canal and docked at Norfolk, Virginia. I was mustered out of the U.S. Navy at their offices on Church Street in New York City. I received an honorable discharge and was authorized to wear a Four-Service Ribbon and three Battle Stars. I returned to my home in Hammonton and applied to the Johns Hopkins Medical School. I also requested an interview with the three members of the Admissions Committee.

5
Medical Education

Vita Breve et Ars Longa

The period of time that I devoted to becoming first a physician and then a general surgeon extended from September 1946 until July 1957. I went to Baltimore, Maryland, soon after I left the navy. I was interviewed by the three members of the Admissions Committee. I saw each one separately. I met Dean Allan McChesney at the dean's medical school office. He was of moderate stature, with light hair and blue eyes and dressed in a dark blue suit. He was pleasant to me but told me, as I expected, that the September 1946 class for admission was filled. He said I could apply for the following year. He observed that my marks at LaSalle College in Philadelphia were not bad, but since they had never had a medical student from my school, they had no yardstick. Abruptly he said, "Why didn't you go to Princeton?" I replied that my parents wanted me to have a good "Catholic college education." He said no more.

The second man on the Admissions Committee was Dr. Lewellys Barker. He was a tall, fair-haired, slim, and rather handsome man, an endocrinologist. I met him at his medical office. He remarked that I had been out of school for three years and I might "brush up" on chemistry. He said chemistry was the "killer course" at Johns Hopkins Medical School.

The third man on the Admissions Committee was Dr. Perrin H. Long. A professor of preventive medicine, he had introduced the sulfa drugs into the United States from France in the mid-thirties. He was very pleasant to me. I met him in his medical school office. He asked me about my wartime naval experience. He said he would help me be admitted to the medical school and would be my adviser if I ever had difficulties. I never had to go to him once in the four years I was at Hopkins. But it was nice to know he was there.

I applied to the Graduate School of the University of Pennsylvania to study biochemistry, physiology, and qualitative organic analysis. I was interviewed by Dr. William Christopher Stade, professor of research medicine, in his office in the Maloney Building on the University of Pennsylvania campus. At first he refused to admit me to the graduate school. He said that I had been out of school too long and should repeat college courses.

I left his office and walked down the hall to the bank of elevators. I was dejected. Suddenly he came out of his office and he called out, "Jannett, come back here!" I went back into his office and he said, "We've changed our mind; you can take any courses you wish in the graduate school and I will be your adviser." I was very happy and I said to him, "I will go at my work tooth and nail; you won't be sorry."

Now I needed a place to live. On the bulletin board in Houston Hall on the University of Pennsylvania campus, I saw a ROOM FOR RENT sign—six and one-half dollars per week and just a short trolley ride from school. I went to 5933 Ellsworth Street one evening and met Miss Margaret M. Murphy, a middle-aged lady of medium stature, light red hair, blue eyes, and fair complexion. She spoke with a strong Irish brogue. Her parents had died and she lived alone. She gave me the front bedroom in the house. It had a bow window, a large oval table, and a lamp. There were two chairs and a large double bed. I was pleased with my accommodations, and she was happy to have someone in the house with her. The fact that I was Catholic and one-half Irish was also in my favor. Miss Murphy, as I always called her, went "to business" each day. She was in charge of the yard goods department at Lit Brothers in Center City.

I began my studies in biochemistry under Dr. David Wright Wilson. The professor of physiology was Dr. Merkel Jacobs. My laboratory instructor in qualitative organic analysis was a young man named John Arnett.

The first day I met Mr. Arnett, he handed me eight organic compounds. The compounds were in test tubes and in either solid or liquid form. We had the task to chemically identify the compounds and prepare two organic compounds from each by the end of the semester.

Returning to schoolwork after three years was difficult. In addition, one day I suffered from first- and second-degree facial burns as a result of an explosive reaction in the laboratory. Only the quick thinking of Mr. Arnett saved me from severe scarring. He washed the area with copious amounts of cool water.

I went home to Hammonton for a few days and was embarrassed to return to school. My old piano teacher had married a good-natured Irishman named Neal Donnelly. He visited me and convinced me to return to school. He drove me back to Philadelphia and my quarters. He was a Good Samaritan.

When I told Miss Murphy that the work was difficult and I had thought of giving up, she said, "Andy, a drop of water at a time will make a hole in a stone."

When I took a test, Miss Murphy would set up an altar to the Blessed Mother in her dining room with flowers and a vigil candle lit. I felt that I could not possibly fail or I might undermine Miss Murphy's faith.

In the chemistry laboratory in the Harrison Building, the man next to me was a veteran air force captain, Jerry Morse, who had been discharged from the service one year before I had. Whenever I had difficulties, he would advise me as to how to proceed in identifying the unknown compounds.

As the Christmas holidays approached, I was progressing well in biochemistry and physiology but had only completed work on four of the "unknowns." Four of my compounds were still "unknown."

I visited Brother Raymond, my old chemistry professor at LaSalle College, and told him that I needed access to a laboratory. He handed me the keys to his lab and said, "Don't blow it up or set it on fire." Also, he warned that the heat would be turned off.

During the two weeks of Christmas vacation, I worked with my overcoat on in the lab. I got snow and ice from out on the street to use to facilitate precipitation of certain compounds.

At the end of the semester, I got seven out of eight of my "unknowns" correct. The one compound I got wrong I called 2-amino, 4 nitrobenzene. The correct answer was 2-amino, 4 nitro-toluene. I missed a Ch_3 methyl-radicle on the benzene ring.

On January 13, 1947, I received a letter of admission to the Johns Hopkins Medical School for the September 1947 class. They required a reading knowledge of French and German. I had studied German for four years at LaSalle but had never been exposed to French. Accordingly, I took two years of French at LaSalle College under the tutelage of Dr. John Guishard.

In September 1947, I matriculated at the Johns Hopkins Medical School. I saw an ad on the bulletin board at the school that told of a room at 3104 Hartford Road in Baltimore. The cost of the room was six and one half-dollars per week, with breakfast daily. About this time, I met a tall young man with a pronounced southern accent. I asked him where he was staying, and he gave the same address where I had arranged quarters for myself. The young man's name was Alex Haller. I had purchased a new Ford with my savings from my navy years. We drove out to meet Mrs. Raymond Kreis, our new landlady.

We found out that a third medical student also lived there. John Bryan Price, a young man from Kilgore, Texas, was to be my roommate for the following year. The three of us drove to school daily from Hartford Road. We joined the Phi Chi Medical Fraternity and took our noon and evening meals there. Martin, an elderly black gentleman, and his assistant, Goldie, looked after all our needs at the fraternity. We all called Martin the Whispering Dream and all laughed together.

The first day at Phi Chi at lunch, I sat next to Gabe Tucker, who was to be my classmate, the person who had been my legal adviser in the Philippine Islands. It truly is a small world.

As I was a veteran, the GI Bill of Rights paid all of my $600-a-year tuition at Hopkins. I received all my books, which were practically new, and $75 per month subsistence. About one-half of my class were World War II veterans. There had been 4,500 applications for admissions to Hopkins Medical School that year, so I felt indeed lucky to be one of 75 accepted.

School started in earnest and gross anatomy, biochemistry, physiology, microscopic anatomy, and neuroanatomy kept us busy. The year I spent at U. of P. was invaluable.

The determination of the pH of the blood required an understanding of the Henderson-Hasslerbach Equation. On one of our first tests in chemistry, we had a question on pH determination. One student answered the pH question with this comment: "Show me a practicing physician in Baltimore who knows the Henderson-Hasslebach equation and I'll show you a green horse." When his paper came back, the professor wrote: "We have not seen a green horse, but we have seen a jackass."

During the school year, about one dozen students dropped out for various reasons. Some did not like dissecting a cadaver, some became ill, and one student left to join the ministry.

We took comprehensive exams at the end of each year and were relieved when we learned that we passed.

The second year of medical school was taken up in good part by gross and microscopic pathology. The acting head of pathology was the brilliant Arnold Rice Rich, M.D. He was famous in medical circles for his original work with such diseases as tuberculosis, periarteritis nodosum, and hypersensitivity. Once per week, he assembled the class for an oral quiz. We each waited with bated breath, hoping we would not be called upon. But we all loved him and admired him for his teaching ability. One of my favorites in the Pathology Department was our instructor,

Dr. Gordon Henniger, a graduate of Dalhousie Medical School in Nova Scotia.

In the spring, Dr. Gordon Henniger would take my group to the New Broadway Hotel and over a stein of beer we discussed pathology. He told us of a patient who drank so much that when he died the liver was so cirrhotic, the doctor had to cut it with a saw.

During the last part of our second year in medical school, we were introduced to physical diagnosis. Now we each had to purchase a stethoscope and an ophthalmoscope. This equipment, plus our long white coats, caused us to feel that we had truly arrived. The teacher of my group was Dr. Joseph Lilienthal, a young professor of environmental medicine. He also taught me in my junior and senior years. Again, comprehensive exams were given at the end of the second year. We never received numerical grades or those with letters of the alphabet. Your grade was either Satisfactory or Unsatisfactory.

When we returned to school in the third year we began to feel like budding clinicians. We each wore a long white coat with a stethoscope in the right pocket and a small black notebook in the left. We entered through the main entrance of the hospital under the "dome." In the rotunda is a large white marble statue of Christ with his arms outstretched, and the legend at the base of the statue reads: "Come to me all ye who labor and are heavily burdened."

Our teachers all tried to emulate the "Great Four Physicians" immortalized in the painting by John Singer-Sargent: Sir William Osler, the first professor of medicine at Hopkins; William Stewart Halstead, the first professor of surgery; Howard A. Kelly, the first professor of obstetrics and gynecology; and William Welch, the first professor of pathology. Their work in the field of medicine set the standards and traditions at Hopkins.

Dr. Alfred Blalock was the professor of surgery during our medical school years. He and Dr. Helen Taussig, a pediatrician, had achieved fame for an operation devised to relieve cyanosis of the congenital abnormalities of the heart. The children so afflicted were known as "blue babies."

We received instruction in the various surgical, medical, and pediatric specialties from full- and part-time physicians. The professors were full-time teachers, who also carried out research projects. The residency system was pyramidal. Several residents started in surgical or medical pursuits, and each year their number was reduced until one senior resident remained. Many men were in residency five or more years. They also assisted in training medical students. It was in my third year of medical school that I delivered a baby for the first time. An obstetrical resident named Dr. Langford was my instructor. The patient was fully draped and appropriately sedated. I was gowned and gloved with cap and mask. Dr. Langford told me to call him when the baby "crowned." Soon the baby crowned. I called out two or three times, "Dr. Langford." But Dr. Langford had planned to be out of the room when I performed my first delivery. During our third year, several of my classmates and I joined the U.S. Army Medical Corps and were commissioned as first lieutenants. We were instructed in military medicine by Col. Byron Steger. The summer of 1950 we were sent to Oliver General Hospital, a military hospital in Augusta, Georgia. We worked as externs and enjoyed playing golf in our free time.

In the fourth year of medical school, we

were responsible for "working up" the patients. We did the history and physical exam and the basic laboratory tests ourselves. Once a week, at "high noon" on Fridays, one of our number was selected to present a case in Hurd Hall. In the first row of the amphitheater, there sat the professor and his entourage of residents and interns. The remaining seats were filled with the upper classes of the medical school. No gladiator in ancient Rome suffered more than the poor student in the "pit" for that week.

In the second half of the fourth year, a medical student was allowed to choose an elective. My best friend, Robert Bruce Hunter, and I decided to become exchange students at the Harvard Medical School in Boston, Massachusetts. We traveled up to Boston in the dead of winter in Bob's old Plymouth, engaged rooms at Vanderbilt Hall, and traveled to Massachusetts General Hospital daily. Bob worked on the Medical Service. I worked as an extern on the West Surgical Service of Dr. Edward Churchill. The chief surgical resident was Dr. William Waddell. I was permitted to "scrub in" as a second assistant on many operations.

As graduation neared, fourth-year students began to apply for internships. I was interested in a good rotating internship, one in which the intern rotates through medical, surgical, pediatric, obstetrical, and other services. After returning from Boston, I secured an appointment for an interview at the Philadelphia General Hospital regarding a rotating internship. About four hundred medical students applied, and ninety-four were accepted. I received my M.D. degree at John Hopkins Homewood Campus on June 12, 1951. Dean Chesney handed us our degrees.

Internship—July 1, 1951, through June 30, 1952

In those days, the Philadelphia General Hospital, also known as "Old Blockley," was a huge complex of buildings on Thirty-fourth Street in Center City, Philadelphia. There were more than two thousand beds and thirty-five hundred employees. It was essentially a hospital for the indigent of the city, although there was a police and firemen section. The administrator was Dr. Pat Lucchesi.

Soon after our arrival, Dr. Lucchesi assembled the new group of ninety-four interns. He announced that discipline and proper behavior on our part was essential. He also warned that no indiscretions so far as the nurses or student nurses were concerned would be tolerated. I was assigned quarters in the doctors' annex, a building adjacent to the Neuropsychiatry Building. My roommate was Dr. Dean Clark, a Californian.

My first assignment was to "Men's Radio." I soon learned that this was code for cancer ward. Most of the patients on Men's Radio were terminal cancer patients. Dr. Bernard Widman was the chief of radiation therapy, and I made rounds with him and his residents. One of his residents was a comely girl, who invited me to a party at the Vesper Boat Club, along the Schuylkill River. It was an affair given to raise money for some charity. The high point of the evening was my introduction to Grace Kelly and her mother. The year was 1951 and Grace Kelly had not made her mark in the movies. She had just appeared in a Broadway play called *The Moon Is Blue*.

I rotated through the medical, surgical,

and pediatric services. Finally, I was assigned to a very busy obstetrics and gynecology service. I delivered ninety-four babies while on this service. One night a very heavy woman suffered a prolapsed umbilical cord in the emergency room. I found that I could only keep the cord pulsating if I applied pressure to the presenting baby's head. The resident ordered me to stay put as we rushed to the operating room. By now, my hand was numb; I called up through the drape sheets, "Be careful not to cut my fingers!" Twin babies were safely delivered.

At this time Philadelphia General Hospital still had an ambulance service and interns were required to do home deliveries. One night about three o'clock in the morning, my phone rang. The cheery operator said, "Good morning, Doctor. How would you like to take a nice early-morning drive?" A lady named Dutch had called to request medical assistance with the birth of her child. Her address had been given to Tony, the ambulance driver. I dressed quickly and ran to the obstetrical department to get the black bag and hoped everything I would need was in the bag. I met the ambulance at the main gate. We sped through the darkened and nearly deserted streets, finally stopping in front of a three-story row house. There were no lights to be seen in the house. I said, "Tony, are you sure this is the right house?"

He said, "Go to the door and ask if there is a lady named Dutch living there and about to deliver a baby."

I went to the door and knocked. An elderly woman came to the door and asked what I wanted. I said that a lady named Dutch had called for medical assistance for home delivery of a baby.

She said, "Just me and the old man live here and no one is going to have a baby." Then she closed the door. I went back to the ambulance and told Tony we had the wrong address. He said we could get the right address from the precinct police station, and we succeeded in that way in getting to the patient's home. I was directed to a small back bedroom and arrived just in time to assist her with the delivery. I noticed that the child was born with a cleft lip and palate. The mother wanted to see her child. I told her we would bring her and the child back to the hospital, since she had suffered a tear of the outlet of the birth canal. This tear could be best repaired in the operating room at the hospital. After Tony, the ambulance driver, and I loaded the mother and child in the ambulance, we returned to the hospital emergency room as the sun was coming up.

The charge nurse in the ER said, "Why are you bringing them back to the hospital? Don't you know that's why we send you out?" I explained the medical problems of the mother and child and the nurse accepted my explanation. Both problems were properly attended to. The state of Pennsylvania had a special program for the repair of cleft lip and palate.

Two other services through which I rotated were metabolic diseases (mostly diabetes) and tuberculosis. A new antibiotic, streptomycin, had been discovered and was now being used in the treatment of tuberculosis. I was always fearful of being infected with tuberculosis since my grandmother had died of this disease and one of my uncles had spent a year in a sanitarium before the disease was arrested.

During my internship, my sister Peggy was newly married, my brother, Albert, was enrolled at the University of Notre Dame, and my younger sister, Kathleen, was a sophomore at St. Joseph's High School in Hammonton. My GI Bill of Rights assistance was coming to an end. I wanted to take a residency in general surgery. A hospital in Akron, Ohio, offered a graded residency in surgery with a generous stipend. At PGH I had worked for twenty-five dollars a month. I accepted an appointment as a surgical resident in Akron. I soon realized that I had made an error in accepting the appointment. I overheard one of the older surgeons telling a colleague, "Don't teach these young ones too much. The first thing you know, they'll be out in competition with us." I left after one year of training.

    At this time, a doctor in Philadelphia had successfully treated a series of cases of scarring of the mitral valve with mitral commissurotomy. He was Charles P. Bailey at Hahnemann Hospital. I applied for a surgical residency at Hahnemann Hospital and Medical College. I was accepted by the professor of surgery, Dr. William L. Martin. He had been chief of surgery at the Philadelphia Naval Hospital during World War II. He was a large, powerful man and when he spoke people listened, especially surgical residents. He was a personal friend of Dr. Charles Mayo of the famous Mayo Clinic.

It was a graded four-year surgical residency. We received room and board, uniforms, and fifty dollars per month. The first year, two other residents and I rotated through the clinics and surgical pathology. In the second year, we rotated on the various surgical services of private practicing surgeons. I especially enjoyed the time I spent on the plastic and neurological surgery services. As residents, we did history and physical exams and ordered various blood tests, X rays, and other tests as directed by the head of each service. Also, we assisted at operations as either first or second assistant.

While on the neurosurgical service, I worked under the direction of a tall, very thin, angular-featured physician of Swedish descent, Dr. Axel Olsen. He had trained at the Lahcy Clinic in Boston. He was a man of few words. During my time on his service, I assisted him in removing twenty-two brain tumors of various types. There were many interesting cases, but one in particular stands out in my memory. A thirty-five-year-old truck driver had stopped at a bar for a cold bottle of beer on a warm summer day. As he stepped off the stool, he stumbled backward and struck the back of his head on a nearby jukebox. Initially, he was taken to St. Joseph's Hospital in Lancaster, Pennsylvania. For three days he remained unconscious before being transferred to our hospital and Dr. Olsen's service in Philadelphia. The truck driver was placed in a quiet environment. Initial X rays of the skull were negative for fracture. Appropriate intravenous therapy and suctioning of the respiratory tract were carried out as he remained in deep coma with no localizing signs. After several days, I made Burr holes on both sides of the skull but found no evidence of subdural hemorrhage. The brain itself was slightly shrunken, so I increased his fluid therapy. Days and then weeks passed. After a month, with the coma persisting, many of my doctor friends said I was wasting my time and the patient, Frank S., would be a "vegetable" as long as he lived. The patient had a devoted wife and three small children at home. I spent a lot of my "time off" with this patient. One evening, I was making an incision on his ankle in search of one of his last remaining veins for fluid therapy. Since he was comatose, I did not use a local anesthetic. As I teased the wound open with a hemostat, I inadvertently stretched a sensory nerve. The patient astounded me and the nurse when he sat bolt upright in bed and blurted out, "What the hell are you doing?" Then he fell back in bed to resume his previous state. I was overjoyed. I redoubled my efforts to correct even the slightest chemical imbalance of his blood. I even transfused blood to bring his red blood cell count near normal. Finally, after more than one month, he awoke. He was completely amnesic. He did not know who he was or where he was. He did not recognize his family. He was attended to daily by physical therapists who taught him to walk. I gave him a notebook and pencils to practice writing the alphabet and numbers. Very elementary books were used to teach him to read. One day, he told me that South Philadelphia High School was going to play a football game against Simon Gratz High School that afternoon. His wife told me that he had attended South Philadelphia High School. Soon thereafter, he told me that he was working for Sears & Roebuck and the hood over the truck engine had struck him on the back of his head. His wife then related that he had worked for Sears before he went into the U.S. Army.

On another morning, while I was making rounds, Frank S. said to me, "What do you want me to do today, Sarge?"

I kiddingly said, "Get a broom and sweep out the battalion office."

When he proceeded to sweep out the nurses' station, the charge nurse was ready to give both of us "what for."

Finally, Frank S. recognized his wife and pictures of his children. He rapidly regained weight and strength. Soon he was ready for discharge. (The only neurological defect that I recall was that he exhibited "jumpy legs." When he crossed one leg over the other, the suspended leg and foot made rapid rhythmic small excursions of involuntary movements.) I accompanied Frank S. and his wife to the front door of the hospital and to his brother's waiting car. I can still see Frank in my mind's eye waving good-bye to me through the rear window of the car.

My next assignment was as a resident on the cardiac surgery service of Dr. Charles P.

Bailey. He was a tall, slightly stooped man of about forty-eight years of age. He had given the infant specialty cardiac surgery a giant boost with the success of his mitral commissurotomy operation. He had reduced the mortality rate for that operation to less then 5 percent. He had become a world-renowned cardiac surgeon. His service was large, and he kept two floors of the hospital filled with patients from all over the world. The overflow of patients waited in a nearby hotel for an open bed in the hospital. Four major cardiac procedures were performed daily five days per week. During my time on the cardiac service, a number of novel procedures began to be used. Among them, were:

1. Hypothermia (reducing body temperature to protect vital organs during surgery).
2. Cardiopulmonary bypass and extracorporeal oxygenation of the blood.
3. Cardioplegia (use of chemical agents to still the heart during bypass).

As my time to work on cardiac surgery neared an end, Dr. Bailey invited me to work two more years to become a cardiac surgeon. It was nearly ten years since I had left the navy and entered medical training. I was weary. So I thanked him for the offer but declined.

My final year of surgical residency consisted of being chief resident on the ward service. We residents were now allowed to make surgical decisions and to perform operations. Once a week, we had a meeting with the senior surgical staff to discuss individual cases.

Near the end of my final year in training, I developed a cough and low-grade fever. Also, I felt very tired. I decided to have my yearly X ray of my chest. A day or two later, a friend who was an X-ray resident came to the surgical clinic to tell me the professor of radiology wanted to see me. When I entered his darkened office, he had all my chest X rays during my four years' residency on the view boxes.

The most recent chest X ray showed a mottling of the lung fields. He said, "You realize the possibilities as well as we do." I asked if I could have further X rays and additional views. He agreed. I had always feared tuberculosis. However within a relatively short time the lung fields cleared completely. It was determined that I had "walking pneumonia," or a viral pnemonitis.

At long last, June 30, 1957, arrived and I decided to enter private practice in Hammonton, New Jersey. My father, being a builder, put up a six-room-and-bath air-conditioned office behind our home on Packard Street. I spent the remainder of the summer of 1957 getting my equipment and furniture for the office and the new enterprise—private practice.

6
Private Practice Years

Homo liber

I was thirty-four years of age when I began private practice in October 1957. My office was well furnished and equipped, and I was $15,000 in debt. I needed hospital privileges to perform surgery. The hospital that I wanted was in Camden, New Jersey; I was told that the staff was "closed"—that is, they had enough general surgeons. I walked into the lobby of Our Lady of Lourdes Hospital in Camden and asked the woman at the information desk if I could see Mother Paracleta, the administrator. Shortly, a tall nun dressed in a long white habit appeared at the front desk. The white garb surrounded her face. Her eyes were wide-set, warm, and alert. There was a suggestion of a smile on her face. She asked what I wanted. I told her I wanted staff privileges in surgery and gave her a summary of my training. She said, "You have honest eyes; you'll be good for my hospital. Consider yourself on the staff."

I said, "I haven't filled out any application papers."

She said, "That's all right; you can catch up with that later." She also suggested that I meet with Dr. Edward G. Osborn, the chief of the surgical department, and later I did.

In those days, it was customary for a new doctor opening his practice to visit the doctors who were already practicing in the community. My reception in most instances was only lukewarm, as I was looked upon as another competitor. The oldest physician in the town assigned me to the emergency and weekend schedule. I kept busy initially with accident cases. Also, I was appointed physician to the local brewer's football team. On Sunday afternoons, I sat on the bench with the football players. After the game, the players tracked mud into my office as I checked them over for cuts, bruises, knee and ankle injuries, dislocated fingers, and an assortment of other injuries. My utility room was stocked with boxes of Ace bandages, rolls of plaster, bandages, and crutches.

My barbershop, Uncle Rock's, was also a

Author's office and home in Hammonton, NJ (1950–1973).

source of new patients. Uncle Rock's son, Gene Santomas, and I were friends since childhood, and he referred many candidates for surgery to me. The physicians in the town were less accommodating. They were fearful when I spoke of a local hospital. One complained, "The first thing you know, the town will fill up with specialists." My routine made for long days, seven days per week. I lived with my parents, and fortunately, my mother took all phone messages, scheduled patients, and did all my bookwork. I arose at daylight, washed, dressed, and ate breakfast. I then drove thirty miles to Our Lady of Lourdes Hospital in Camden and checked in with Marie Zuzga, the hospital's physiotherapist. Mother Paracleta had appointed me as the physician for the physiotherapy department. I tried to schedule any surgery I had to perform for seven-thirty or eight o'clock in the morning. Then I made rounds on any patients that I had admitted. On my way out of the hospital, I checked in at the physiotherapy department. I then drove back to Hammonton for lunch. From two to four in the afternoon I rested. Then I showered, ate supper, and started evening office hours. In addition, I taught third-year medical students on Saturday mornings. I made up exams and marked them in my spare time. This latter enterprise was helpful to me in preparing for my general surgery board exams. Occasionally I was called to perform an emergency procedure at the Ancora State Hospital. Needless to say, my social life was nil.

My sister Peggy and her family visited us occasionally from North Jersey. My brother, Al, worked with my father in the masonry business, and Al and his young family were frequent visitors. My youngest sister, Kathleen, had graduated from Immaculata College in Washington and then the Tobe Coburn School of Fashion Design. She worked in New York and visited us when her schedule permitted.

The practice grew by leaps and bounds, and soon I was inundated with patients. A large part of my practice was general practice, which further alienated me from the general practitioners. My fees were reasonable. It was five dollars for an office visit, and I frequently dispensed medicine to those whom I felt needed it. The town pharmacist told me that physician dispensing had gone out with "high-button shoes." One day two members of the Rotary Club in a neighboring town came to my office to ask if I would help to find twenty-five members in Hammonton. Soon we were chartered and Dr. Edward George, a radiologist, became the first president. The Rotary Club met one evening a week at the Central Cafe on Third Street. One night after dinner, a few members complained that our club should have some purpose. I told them that nine persons had died during the past summer on the White and Black Horse Pikes as a result of accidents near our town and suggested the need for a small community hospital to take care of accidents and provide a place where local women could have their children. The idea was received with enthusiasm in our club but not in all quarters. Steps were taken to enlist the efforts of the citizenry of the town to promote the building of the hospital, which stands today adjacent to the Hammonton Lake on the White Horse Pike.

I practiced alone for the first five years. Then a fortuitous circumstance happened to alleviate me of general practice. A recently graduated osteopathic physician, Dr. Alex Rodi Sr., joined me in practice. He was and is an excellent physician. This relief gave me a chance to study for and pass my general surgery board examinations in Philadelphia. About this same time, I presented 100 major surgical case results in Atlantic City to Drs. Altman, Mason, and Stewart for admission to the American College of Surgeons.

In the early days of my practice penicillin was still a miracle medicine. Patients and some physicians looked upon it as a panacea for all their ills. Some people would call on the telephone and ask if they could stop by for a "shot of penicillin." Other antibiotics came on the market such as streptomycin, aureomycin, and terramycin, but none achieved the same popularity among the public as penicillin.

One night, early in my career, a forty-eight-year-old baker came to my office with the complaint of recurrent vomiting. The vomit contained flecks of blood. The baker, Lodie P., was a small man and very emaciated. There was a palpable tumor on his upper abdomen. He was admitted to Lourdes Hospital for studies. The X rays of his stomach revealed a huge tumor involving the distal two-thirds of that organ. In surgery, I removed the involved portion of the stomach and as many lymph nodes as I saw in the area. To supplement the small remnant of stomach, I constructed a "pouch" of small intestine to increase the reservoir for food. His progress after surgery was slow. His weight was only 113 pounds. The diagnosis was Hodgkin's disease.

About this time, one of my patients with coronary artery disease invited me to go to Florida with him for a vacation. I agreed to go with him if he would share the expenses for my patient Lodi on the same trip. I told him my patient had eleven children and had never had a vacation. The three of us motored to Florida and stayed at a famous beachfront hotel in Miami Beach. Each night we went to well-known Italian restaurants. Lodi loved Italian food and ate heartily. The patient who had agreed to pay one-half the expenses was amazed, as was I. "I thought you said Lodi didn't eat much," he said. Each day Lodi and I went into the pool and I rubbed him down with suntan lotion. Two weeks later we returned to New Jersey. Lodi was brown as a berry. He now weighed 126 pounds. His wife and children were delighted. He went on to live twenty more years.

Another interesting case early in my career was that of "Kitty A." She was a forty-year-old mother of three children. Her complaints were headaches and the onset of convulsive seizures at age thirty-eight. She gave a history of having struck the right side of her head at an amusement park some twenty years before. She had been rendered unconscious at the time. The young man who assisted her that day she later married. I suggested that she have some skull X rays. She said she had been in three different hospitals in Philadelphia and none of the previous studies "showed anything." She had been taking anticonvulsant medicines for two years. She agreed to be admitted to Lourdes for study. X rays of the skull now revealed a calcified plum-sized mass in the right cerebral hemisphere. I requested a neurosurgical consult. The young brain surgeon refused to operate. He said the tumor was too close to the "motor strip" and surgery might paralyze her on one side. I then ordered a neurosurgical consult from a professor in one of the Philadelphia medical schools. He also declined to operate. I sent the patient home but told her not to give up hope. I summarized the case and sent a letter to Dr. A. Earle Walker, professor of neurosurgery at Johns Hopkins Hospital in Baltimore. He called me on the phone and said he would admit her. New techniques would outline the exact size of the tumor in all planes. After admission, he decided to operate. He invited me to be present at the operation. I got into my car at 5:30 A.M. and arrived at 8:00. A calcified meningioma was successfully removed by 10:30 A.M. Other than a small visual field defect in one eye, there were no deficits. She was able to discontinue her anticonvulsant medications. The patient died many years later of an unrelated disease.

In 1963, I took a motor trip across the United States. My parents and my sister Kathleen accompanied me. We visited Yellowstone National Park and the Seattle, Washington, World's Fair. We traveled along the coast of Oregon and then through Sequoia National Park in California. We visited relatives living in Southern California. Kathleen flew back to New York from Los Angeles. My parents and I returned to New Jersey by the southern route. Arriving home, my father said, "I could go on another trip like that starting tomorrow."

Toward the end of the year 1963, two events stand out in my mind. In the early afternoon of November 23, I was sitting in the barber chair of Uncle Rock's shop. My friend and barber was cutting my hair. We were chatting, as was our custom. The radio was playing low in the background. Suddenly Gene, another barber, stopped his work and moved closer to the radio, the comb and scissors still in his hands. He blurted out, "Andy, they shot the president in the head." Gene turned up the volume of the radio. He added, "He's being raced to the hospital."

I said, "If he's been shot in back of the head, he's probably already dead." Unfortunately, the president had indeed been assassinated. When I returned home, I told my sister Kathleen and she began to cry. We turned on our television to get more details of the tragedy.

The second event occurred a few days later when my youngest sister, Kathleen, married Dr. Ward Curran, an economist. They were married in New York City and spent their honeymoon in Europe.

During the following year, the chief of surgery at Our Lady of Lourdes Hospital suffered a heart attack. While he was still a bed patient in the hospital, he called me to talk. He announced that I would have to start taking emergency calls in Camden. I said that I didn't have an office in that city. He replied that I should get one. He also told me that I would have to cover for him at the Ancora State Hospital until he recovered. But for the next number of years he was ill more often than he was well.

About this time, I was passing through

Author's office and home in Haddonfield, NJ (1973–1990), a Romanesque Victorian, built in 1876.

Haddonfield and observed a FOR SALE sign in front of a large Victorian house at 109 Kings Highway West. The large sign read: "Ideal investment, four apartments and doctor's office." I thought that the location was excellent and there was sufficient parking behind the house. After some dickering over price, I purchased the property in August 1965 for $41,500. I put $10,000 down and assumed a mortgage for the remainder at 5.5 percent interest. I considered myself very fortunate until I learned of repairs needed. The house had been built around 1876 and was a Romanesque Victorian home with a large wrap-around porch with thirteen tall, round columns. The entrance was rounded and a balustrade surmounted it. There were twenty-five rooms, five of which were bathrooms.

I made arrangements to share the doctor's office with Dr. J. Stannard Davis, who was already there. He was a fine gentleman and we got along well for several years, until he suffered a heart attack and retired.

Eventually I emptied the entire building and installed a new heating system with five zones controlled by individual thermostats. Also, I modernized the five bathrooms. One of my patients, Leonard Turreen, lost his job and I employed him for two years, five days a week, to paper and paint and do various other jobs as they turned up. Fortunately, my practice was growing and permitted me to finance the projects at the Victorian home.

On February 17, 1966, at 7:00 A.M., my father died suddenly with a stroke. My mother awakened me out of a sound sleep and said, "Something has happened to your father." I attempted cardiopulmonary resuscitation, but when I saw that my father's pupils were fixed and dilated I ceased all efforts. Marinelli's Funerary on North Third Street in Hammonton handled the subsequent funeral. At the viewing, friends and neighbors passed for nearly four hours offering condolences to my mother and our family.

My mother loved to drive, and in 1967 I purchased a new car for her. She loved to go shopping and visit my father's sister daily to see if she needed anything. Frequently they went to the malls together. From childhood, my mother was very religious, and she visited the church daily in the afternoon.

Meanwhile, the practice of medicine was changing. With the institution of Medicare in 1965 and Medicaid a few years later, there was a tendency to hospitalize patients and order a whole array of studies that would not have been done when the patient himself had to reach into his pocket to pay for them. Also, the free clinics in all hospitals were closed down and physicians with affluent practices refused to accept Medicaid patients because of lower fees.

Today we hear threats of "two-tiered" practice of medicine and "rationing" of medical care. Before Medicare and Medicaid older physicians treated all comers for a reasonable fee or none at all if the patient could not afford it. Hopeless cases of terminal cancer were not kept alive in intensive-care units for weeks on end.

Shortsighted mayors closed great hospitals for the indigent in major cities. These closures, such as that of Philadelphia General, created vacuums in the care of persons not covered by Medicare or Medicaid. Another factor was the increasing threats of malpractice suits by unscrupulous lawyers.

When I started practice in 1957, my insurance premium was $250.00/year. When I left private practice in 1973 the premium had risen to $3500.00/year, and now, in 1992, in many instances the cost is over $100,000. I had never had a malpractice suit in my private practice, and still the company that covered me and preferred risks ultimately went into liquidation. In 1957, the year I entered practice, a chest X ray was $3.00, a room on the ward was $11.50/day. A doctor's fee for a delivery was $150. Today, the costs of the aforementioned items are at least ten times more.

During the latter years of my private practice, I was appointed by leaders of the county medical society to meet with lawyers of the plaintiff and the insurance companies. There were three doctors: an internist, an orthopedist, and myself, a general surgeon. We were able to differentiate spurious cases from those indicating a legitimate need for redress. This procedure avoided long and costly court battles.

At the Ancora State Psychiatric Hospital, a foreign-educated female physician was negligent in the care of a forty-two-year-old woman who had been admitted with depression. The depression had followed the patient's mother's death. The patient also gave a history of a peculiar episode of intravascular clotting and a hospital admission for that condition. Shortly after the patient's admission to the Ancora Hospital, she complained of pain in her right leg. Each time, over the ensuing days, that the young resident was called for the patient's complaint, she ordered medications for relief of the pain. The leg became pale in color and pulseless. When I was finally called to see the patient, she was toxic, with a fever above 104 degrees and her diabetes out of control. After some efforts to stabilize the patient, a right midthigh amputation was performed to remove the gangrenous leg and save the patient's life. Everyone, including myself, was named in a negligence lawsuit. The attorney general's office asked if I would testify in favor of the state. I replied that I would not since the leg might have been salvaged if I had been called much earlier. The legislature of New Jersey met in special session and appropriated a sum of money to permit an out-of-court settlement.

In 1969, my mother and I went on vacation to Italy. We went with a group of members of the N.J. chapter of the Knights of Columbus. We stayed at the Hilton Hotel in Rome. In the south of Italy, we visited Naples, Pompeii, and Sorrento. In the north, we visited Tivoli, some hill towns such as Orvieto and Florence. My mother was especially thrilled with visiting the Vatican and seeing the pope, who at that time was Paul VI.

Also in 1969, I filled the Victorian home in Haddonfield with new renters. Two of the families would stay for more than twenty years. The apartments were large and refurbished and the rents very modest. My mother insisted that I keep the rents low since the people were elderly and on Social Security.

In 1970, our vacation took us to Ireland in the month of May. Our party consisted of my mother and myself, my mother's brother, Bernard, and his wife, Alice. Also on this trip were their son, Tony, and my mother's oldest sister, Mary. We landed at Shannon Airport in Ireland and picked up our Volkswagen van. The van comfortably held six passengers and our luggage. Over the following three weeks, we covered twenty-three hundred miles. We covered the entire periphery of the Emerald Isle and finally came down through the central towns and villages. While there we met many Loughmans, Harringtons, and dozens of cousins. We were invited to parties and dinners, and we all enjoyed a fine visit.

Upon returning home, I received a visit from Mrs. Irma Adams, who had served as the postmistress for many years before retiring. She had learned that developers planned a very large HUD project, encompassing nearly 400 apartments. Knowing that our water and sewer departments were already overburdened, we organized a "Concerned Citizens of Hammonton" group. The cost of educating each child in our school system was also a concern. We were not against slow, orderly growth in our community.

One of the developers told me, "You have a nice, quiet, peaceful little town without much crime."

I answered, "Yes, and those of us who were born and raised here want to keep it that way."

The developers would buy a piece of farmland for a low price. Then they would apply to the town planning and zoning boards for a change in designation for the land to residential.

The valuation of the original farm tract would increase in valuation three- and fourfold. The members of the planning and zoning boards were frequently builders, realtors, and bankers. These individuals could benefit from the new development in a variety of ways. The Concerned Citizens of Hammonton soon heard of the problems that had been left by the developers in other South Jersey communities. With the aid of our attorneys, the development was delayed and finally aborted. It should be revealed that during this controversy the lives of my mother and myself were threatened. But we were not deterred.

There were three interesting cases that I cared for during the last years I was in private practice in Hammonton. I saw hundreds of patients each month, but these three left a lasting impression on my memory.

The first case was that of a fifty-five-year-old man who was building an extra room on his house on a Sunday morning. He came into the emergency room with a towel wrapped around his left wrist. He had accidentally sawed more than halfway through his left arm just above the wrist. He had had a heart attack some weeks before and was on blood thinners. Thus the bleeding was profuse. Also, he had eaten a full breakfast prior to the accident. Under regional anesthesia and tourniquet control, repair of the median nerve, the radial artery, and all the damaged flexor and extensor tendons was carried out. A *Gray's Anatomy* book was placed on a pedestal and referred to frequently during the three-and-one-half-hour procedure. Healing occurred without infection. Physiotherapy restored strength and function. It took about one year for sensation to return to his fingertips. His hand was restored to full function.

The second case that I recall also came in through the emergency room at Our Lady of Lourdes Hospital, about two o'clock in the morning, with no palpable pulse or blood pressure. He had been the victim of a dynamite explosion. His right leg had been blown off below the knee, and one-half of his left foot was found in the shoe four hundred feet away from the accident scene. The patient was a thirty-three-year-old bartender who had noticed a smoking bag that had been placed near the building that he was leaving. When he opened the bag, he realized it contained sticks of dynamite. He dropped the bag and was trying to run when the explosion occurred. Unbeknownst to the patient, his boss had been having trouble with the union. We restored the patient's blood pressure to levels that permitted debridement of his wounds in the operating room. I called an orthopedist to help me. We packed the wounds open and took cultures, since the wounded areas had been impregnated with earth and hedge leaves. In spite of heavy antibiotic therapy, the patient developed gas gangrene a few days after the accident. We transferred the patient to St. Barnabus Hospital in northern New Jersey for hyperharic oxygen therapy, which proved successful. The patient was returned to Camden for revision of the amputation stumps and skin grafts. The patient was fitted with appropriate prosthetics and taught to ambulate again with lightweight crutches. Later his eardrums were replaced to improve his hearing. About one year later, he returned to work as a bartender at his previous place of employment.

In the fall of 1972, a tall, very thin, Roman Catholic priest was referred to my office in Haddonfield. Physical exam revealed a very large tumor of the stomach, which explained his digestive complaints and emaciation. My working diagnosis was cancer of the stomach. Studies at Our Lady of Lourdes Hospital revealed a large tumor involving the distal two-thirds of the stomach, which permitted slow egress of the barium meal. I explained to the patient and the referring physician that the tumor was advanced in nature. They both said, "Do the best you can." The night before the day of surgery, I visited the priest and explained the operation I hoped to be able to perform. I assured him that if the tumor was not removable, I would give him a special diet and medicine to relieve discomfort. The operation was scheduled for nine o'clock in the morning. I arrived at the OR one half hour early to gown and "scrub up" so that no time would be lost. Shortly before nine o'clock, the head operating room nurse told me that the priest was not coming down because he and the doctor—that is, myself—had not done something. I broke scrub, put on a long white coat, and went up to the sixth floor to his room, 615. As I entered, I said, "Father, what is it that we haven't done?"

He replied, "We haven't prayed together."

I warned him that he had had premedication and if he tried to get out of bed, he might fall and hit his head. In spite of my warning, he arose from bed and stood barefoot in front of me. He placed both of his hands on the top of my head. As I stood motionless, he prayed to the Holy Spirit. He continued as follows: "Open my surgeon's mind and guide his hands so that I may have a successful outcome."

We both made the sign of the cross, and he returned to bed. As I left the room, my arms felt like lead and I thought, *He just does not understand. Even if the tumor is operable, gastric cancer yields a less than 5 percent five-year survival.*

At surgery, the tumor was large and very hard except for the upper one-third of the stomach. I took a biopsy and sent it down to the pathology department. The report came back quickly: "Anaplastic cancer." I said to the nurse, "That's the worst form of cancer; the tumor is fixed. Give me the closing suture." As I began to close the abdominal wall, the thought struck me like being hit in the forehead with the end of a two-by-four: *If you don't try, he has no chance at all.* I handed the OR nurse the closing suture and asked for the dissecting scissors and forceps. Two hours later, I had resected the lower two-thirds of the stomach and had joined the remaining portion to the small bowel.

Following surgery, I called the referring general practitioner on the telephone. I told him I had been able to remove most of the cancer and that the liver appeared and felt normal.

After several days the priest was discharged from the hospital. He came once a week to my office for vitamin injections. I used multivitamin B and C, plus 1,000 milligrams of vitamin B12. About three months after surgery, he asked if he could play tennis. I said, "Why not, if you feel up to it?" I should mention that the patient received no X rays or chemotherapy. Ten years after his surgery, I had the opportunity to have breakfast with the priest. He had gained considerable weight, and his color was good. He was eating oatmeal, toast, and coffee. After the meal, I examined his abdomen and found no liver enlargement. There was no enlargement of lymph nodes in neck, axillae or groins. Twenty years later, I had the privilege of hearing the priest say mass. The age of miracles is not over. They happen in each one of our lives if we will only stop, look, and listen and recognize them when they occur. The priest is now approaching his eightieth year.

In the early part of 1973, as I approached my fiftieth birthday, I decided to retire from private practice. There were a number of reasons for my decision. First of all, driving back and forth to the hospital daily for sixteen years, plus the burdens of a heavy schedule, made me weary. The daily driving distance was sixty miles. I had office hours in Hammonton and Haddonfield, and a twenty-five-mile distance separated the two. Another consideration was the rising cost of malpractice insurance. Although I had never had a malpractice suit in my own private practice, there was always the fear that I could have now.

    At nights when I was on emergency call in Our Lady of Lourdes Hospital in Camden, I sometimes had to leave my mother alone in a large house with daily office receipts and narcotic drugs. This was no small concern on my part. When I went into the OR in the middle of the night, I would call my mother when I first arrived at the hospital and when the operation was over. I always made sure the garage door was down when I left home, so that no one would know she was alone. I began to curtail my practice and to refer patients to other specialists if the course of treatment promised to be long. Many of my patients with a history of breast cancer or the like were referred to the Fox Chase Cancer Center for long-term follow-up. This center was in Philadelphia.

Preparations were made to sell my home and office in Hammonton to another physician and surgeon. In September 1973, I wrote a letter of resignation from the staff of Our Lady of Lourdes Hospital. My mother received the money from the sale of our home and office in Hammonton. The two of us moved into one of the apartments of my home in Haddonfield. I was uncertain about what I would do with the remaining portion of my professional life, but I felt relieved of the heavy burdens that private practice of medicine and surgery entails. Medicine had changed considerably since 1957. Medicare came into being in 1965. The New Jersey Medicaid program came along in 1969. Third-party carriers began to dictate to physicians which patients could be admitted to a hospital, how long they could stay, and what fee would be paid. Particularly galling was the fact that in many instances the persons making these decisions were not even physicians.

I continued to work as a surgical consultant at the Ancora State Mental Hospital. I must admit that I missed private practice at first. I missed my patients, my fellow physicians, and many of the nurses at the hospital.

7
Pony Express Physician

Sometime during the spring of 1974, I saw an advertisement in the *Journal of the American Medical Association*. The U.S. Air Force was seeking physicians and especially specialists for their hospitals in Europe, Japan, and other parts of the globe. I applied for a position as a surgeon in an air force hospital in Germany. It took nearly a year for my background check by some thirty-six government agencies, including the Internal Revenue Service.

In April 1975, I was named surgeon for the Thirty-sixth Tactical Fighter Wing in Bitburg, Germany. I was given the rank of full colonel. The program was called Pony Express Physicians. Before going to Germany, I attended an indoctrination course at Lackland Air Base in Texas. Having been a commissioned officer in the U.S. Navy during World War II facilitated my reentrance into the military.

My mother accompanied me to Germany as my dependent. We departed from McGuire Air Force Base at Fort Dix, New Jersey. We arrived in Frankfurt, Germany, early on a gloomy rainy morning. The chief of the obstetrics and gynecology department, a Col. Nicholas Parapid, and two enlisted men met us. It took a number of hours to drive from Frankfurt to Bitburg, a small town near the Luxembourg border. During the trip, my sponsor, Colonel Parapid, said he had a little "bad news." The news was that he had been unable to find a place for my mother and me to live. So, upon arrival at the air force base in Bitburg, my mother and I lived in the VIP officers' quarters for a few weeks, until we were given an apartment.

I selected furniture from a large warehouse on the base. We had serviceable appliances and a television set. I had to purchase special transformers to adapt the electric current to our appliances. Our apartment was in a complex of three-story sand-colored stucco buildings. The inhabitants were jokingly called Cliff Dwellers. Across from our apartment house, there was a shopping center and, most important for my mother, a chapel. She and I attended mass together each afternoon at five o'clock. The Catholic chaplain was Major Mullens.

The air force hospital at Bitburg was an eighty-five-bed one-story facility that had been built by the French government after World War II. The hospital commander was Col. Donald Harmon. He was of medium height, sandy-haired, blue-eyed, and quick-moving. He also was a veteran of World War II, where he had served in the U.S. Navy. I was made the chief of surgery and was also placed in charge of the emergency room. I was given a small radio nicknamed the Brick, and my designated station call was "White Portable One." Over the next twenty-seven months that I served in Germany, I heard the call many dozens of times, "White Portable One, this is Hospital Control. Report to the emergency room at once."

Our patients were mostly young white male pilots, mechanics, and airmen of various rates. We in the Medical Corps also took care of the dependents, women and children. During the summer months, we cared for any American national in an emergency situation. Also, there were a fair number of retirees and their families. These retirees were mostly retired air force officers who had married German women. Occasionally we took care of employees of the American embassy in Luxembourg.

The complement of the hospital staff consisted at the time of my arrival of twenty-seven medical doctors, a like number of nurses, X-ray and laboratory technicians, and Medical Corpsmen and physiotherapy technicians. Many of the ancillary personnel were German nationals. We all got along very well in our daily work. As the chief of surgery, I performed many operative procedures under my own service but was called upon to assist other specialists in ear, nose, and throat, orthopedics, cesarian sections, and other procedures. Duty hours were from 8:00 A.M. to 5:00 P.M. I usually joined my mother for lunch hour unless I had an emergency.

In the evenings I frequently took my mother for a drive through the countryside. In May and June, the orchards were in bloom and the countryside around Bitburg was like a giant garden. Some evenings, we visited Trier, a city eighteen miles south of Bitburg, or Vianden, a town in Luxembourg seventeen miles to the east. We stopped at little ancient stone chapels and said a prayer or lit a candle. I had purchased a new Ford Granada car, so I felt safe to travel. The car agency was across the road from the air force base.

On weekends, when I was off duty, my mother and I frequently took longer trips to Liege, Belgium, or Cologne or Bonn. We especially enjoyed traveling along the Rhine River from Koblenz to Bingen. My mother had a hobby of collecting Hummels, and she had made friends with a merchant named Kissinger who had a store in Bacharach. He used to give her a 15 percent discount, as she was a good customer.

Since my mother had many hours to while away, I encouraged her to join the German, French, and American Wives' Club. Through this club, she visited religious shrines, such as Lourdes, Nevers, and Parais Le Moniel. At Christmastime, she went with the club to Nuremberg to see the shops with their toys and decorations.

Around Christmastime of 1975, I received the news that the air force thought my mother had too much income to be my dependent. They informed me that I had to move off-base and live on the German economy. Accordingly, I found a nice apartment with three bedrooms in the town of Bitburg. I then had to shop in the German markets at greater expense to me. I tried to explain that I had cared for my mother since my father's death in 1966. When they denied my plea, I informed them that since I was unaccompanied by a dependent, my obligation to serve in Europe would be only two years rather than four. The officials for the air force accepted my argument.

As a colonel, I could afford to live on the German economy, but many of the enlisted personnel with families were hard pressed financially.

During one Christmas season, an enlisted man, his wife, and their two children became ill with heavy colds. They lived in a village called Prüm, eighteen miles north of the base in Bitburg. Their house was cold and drafty. Their food supply was scant and their old car inoperative. The hospital commander was away, and I was in charge in his absence. Since it was Christmastime, many of the hospital beds were open. I sent an ambulance to Prüm to pick the family up for admission to the hospital. They enjoyed the warmth of the hospital and the personnel. Needless to say, they enjoyed a fine turkey dinner on Christmas Day.

When the hospital commander returned, he asked me, "What was their admitting diagnosis?"

I replied, "Pneumonia." Nothing more was said.

During the twenty-seven months I served in Europe, my mother and I entertained several of her grandchildren and my two sisters and their husbands. On separate occasions and in small groups we would make a trip to Paris, then to Luzern, Switzerland, Feldskirk, Austria, through the Black Forest, Baden Baden, and back home to Bitburg.

The high point of our stay abroad was a visit to the Holy Land of Israel. My mother and I, although Catholic, joined a Baptist group on a religious pilgrimage. We arrived with Bibles and read passages at such places as Jerusalem, Bethlehem, Nazareth, Jericho, Tiberias, and the Sea of Galilee. We visited many historic places such as the Dead Sea and Masada and the Gaza Strip. There was a Baptist hospital in Gaza, and the administrator asked me to work there for a year. I told him that I owed the U.S. Air Force one more year of service.

During my time in the Middle East, I visited Amman, Jordan, the ancient city of Petra, about one hundred miles south of Amman, and the overpopulated city of Cairo, Egypt. A few miles from Cairo, we visited the Great Pyramids. My mother, age seventy-one, insisted on climbing 445 feet inside the pyramid of the pharaoh Cheops.

We were amazed at the remarkable state of preservation of the paintings inside the tombs. We were impressed by the magnitude and number of granite burial crypts for the sacred bulls of the ancient Egyptians.

After returning to work at the air force hospital in Bitburg, I recall two cases of unusual interest. The first case involved a thirty-three-year-old dependent of German descent. She gave a history of having taken birth control pills for a long period before developing a tumor of her liver. A year before she came under my observation, she had undergone exploratory surgery. The operative report described the location of an inoperable liver tumor, and the pathology report of the liver biopsy described its malignant nature.

When I explored her abdomen because of a nonfunctioning gallbladder a year after the first operation, the liver tumor had completely disappeared. She had been off the birth control pill for more than a year. She was amazed and gratified.

The second case was that of a pleasant, middle-aged black woman. She also was a dependent of a serviceman. She presented with a very large tumor in her abdomen. At first it was not clear what organ gave rise to the enormous growth. A gynecologist assured me that it did not arise from the pelvic organs. At operation, the tumor was found to arise from the right lobe of the liver. Using rubber shod clamps and many homeostatic sutures, we were able to remove the mass. Fortunately, the pathology report was benign. The patient made an uneventful recovery.

During the early part of 1977, I received a letter from the Department of Health and Human Services of New Jersey. The letter had been forwarded to me from my Haddonfield address. A review of my record at Ancora State Hospital had been made, and I was offered a position as a consultant in the New Jersey Medicaid program. I filled out the appropriate application forms and promised to present myself for an interview in the month of June.

I was discharged from the air force in Europe in mid-May 1977. My mother and I toured France. We visited the great cathedrals of Rheims, Auxerre, Orleans, Chartres, Tours, and Mont San Michele. One day we passed through a small town and saw many cars surrounding a church. It was early afternoon. My mother suggested that we hear mass. I parked the car and we went into church. An usher escorted me to a bench in the front of the crowded church. It was to be a funeral mass, and the usher had mistaken me for a member of the family. The casket of the deceased was in the aisle between the front benches. The eulogy extolled the virtues of Madame Fanelle. She apparently had been a pillar of the community, religious, kind, charitable. As the mass neared completion, my mother whispered in my ear, "Can we leave early?"

"No," I replied. "We are sitting with the

family; we must do whatever they do or we'll make a scene."

At the end of the mass, each member of the family and my mother and I sprinkled the casket with holy water and filed past a basket on the altar to leave a donation. I donated for the both of us.

We also visited a number of famous châteaus in the Loire Valley, such as Chambourd.

On Memorial Day, we visited Omaha Beach and the cemetery of Saint Hilaire, where thousands of American soldiers are buried. My father used to tell the story of an eighteen-year-old soldier who was in a dugout with him in the closing days of World War I. They were under German bombardment. The young soldier wanted to go out of their shelter to relieve himself. My father warned him to stay put. He went to leave and no sooner got topside than he was hit and killed instantly.

The St. Hilaire Cemetery was well maintained, and the officials in the office found the date of Private Weber's death—October 18, 1918—and his gravesite. My mother and I said a prayer in the gray granite chapel and departed.

On June 6, 1977, the *Queen Elizabeth II* docked at Cherbourg, France. My car was suspended in air and steam-cleaned of all dirt and placed aboard. My mother and I were pleased with our adjoining staterooms. The size and grandeur of the ship were matched by the excellent service and concern for the passengers.

The crossing of the Atlantic was smooth, and the weather was pleasant. We landed in New York on June 11, 1977. The morning was sunny and pleasant after going through customs; my car was placed on the pier. I packed our luggage in the trunk and headed for Trenton, New Jersey, and an interview at the Department of Health and Human Services on State Street. When I arrived there I met Dr. Jesse W. Carl, whom I had known at Johns Hopkins. He was a urology resident when I was a third-year medical student. Now he was the regional medical consultant in southern New Jersey.

My interview went well. The medical director was Dr. Charles Breme. He asked me if there was anything in my background that could be embarrassing to the department or myself. I said, "I was investigated by thirty-six government agencies in the year before I was commissioned a colonel in the U.S. Air Force." The day after my interview he called me at nine o'clock in the morning and asked when I could start work in the Camden Medicaid Office.

Before leaving the subject of my service in the air force, I had a pleasant surprise a few weeks after I arrived stateside. I received the Air Force Commendation Medal and a citation to accompany the award. It ended with: "The distinctive accomplishments of Col. Jannett reflect credit upon himself and the United States Air Force."

8
Medical Consultant, New Jersey Medicaid Program (July 1977–September 1983)

I was assigned to the Camden County Medicaid Office on Cooper Street in Camden City. My office was spacious and on the second floor of a beautiful stone building. My duties included review of the medical needs of some seventy thousand recipients in the Camden County District. Each day, starting at 8:00 A.M., I would review the files and requests of the recipients for nursing home care, medications, transportation to and from medical facilities, prostheses such as artificial legs and eyes, nursing care in the home, and many other needs too numerous to mention.

The position required that I approve or reject the request after careful consideration of the real medical need. My training of four years at Johns Hopkins Medical School, a year of internship at Philadelphia General Hospital, five years of surgical residency, sixteen years in private practice, and two years of military medicine gave me the background to make an honest and fair judgment in each and every case.

My immediate supervisor in the Medicaid program was Dr. Jesse W. Carll, who was a retired obstetrician and gynecologist from Bridgeton, New Jersey. He was the regional director, and his office was in the Labor Department Building on Landis Avenue in Vineland, New Jersey. We had a good working relationship and consulted almost daily on the telephone. The Medicaid program in southern New Jersey had two other offices, one of which was located in Atlantic City and the other in the Southwood Shopping Center in Woodbury. During the first few years that I was with the program, we had a third physician in Atlantic City. He was an old-time retired general practitioner named Dr. Claude Sullivan. A graduate of the University of Alabama, he was very proud of the "Crimson Tide" football team. It was a pleasure to consult with Claude. He was very wise, knowledgeable, and most of all, blessed with common sense.

We worked each day till 5:00 P.M. five days a week. Occasionally we made house calls to make on-site review of a patient's need for oxygen supplies, nursing needs, etcetera. Also, we made "off-hours" inspections of nursing homes to see how care was rendered at times other than scheduled visits.

The physicians in the program saved funds many times their modest salary over the course of a year. Many requests were rejected when the need cited was downright foolish or ridiculous, and occasionally unscrupulous doctors made requests that were only beneficial to themselves. For example, a patient would ask for twelve miles' transportation at a cost of $100 to have his teeth cleaned. I told this able-bodied ambulatory man that a bus passed in front of his house, which would take him to his dentist. A podiatrist might request "walking shoes" for an infant who was not sitting up, let alone walking. When I called the doctor's attention to this fact, he apologized.

There were many bizarre and unusual

requests for services. One lady had had two abortions paid for by Medicaid, and then her Fallopian tubes were tied to prevent further pregnancies. This latter procedure was also paid for by the Medicaid program. "Now," said she "I want to get my tubes untied." I explained to her that at that time chances of success of the procedure were remote. She decided to forgo the procedure.

Prior to my employment at the Camden Medicaid Office, a young father of three children had been approved by the program for "Sexual Reassignment"—that is, surgical transformation from male to female. During my tenure, another young man came to the office one day requesting removal of facial hair by electrolysis prior to sexual reassignment. I explained that I could not approve his request until several physicians, including psychiatrists, reviewed his medical history. He decided to pay his own expenses in order to avoid "red tape."

There were occasions when the rules were bent a little. A mother of four children had been deserted by her husband. She went to real-estate school and obtained her license to sell property. She phoned one day requesting a new pair of shoes. She explained that she was ashamed to go to her office with her old ones. The law required that there had to be a deformity of the feet in order to supply shoes. Although her feet were normal, we made up a diagnosis. Sometime later, she called me to say that she and her children were no longer on Medicaid or Welfare. She had been successful in her work, and she added, "It all started with a new pair of shoes."

One day, a young man, quite tall and good-looking except for very prominent and protruding ears, came in. Although cosmetic surgery was not allowed, we approved "reconstruction" of his ears. Much later he called to say he was a state trooper.

There were many heart-rending cases that we reviewed for their medical needs: elderly parents in nursing homes, wives abandoned by their husbands and the fathers of their children, young girls abused by stepfathers, and young men who suffered from severe sports injuries, paralyzed from the neck down.

As a medical consultant, I visited a number of the Medicaid offices in the lower third of the state. One cold, wintry morning after a recent blizzard, I was working in the Woodbury Medicaid Office. The phone rang and a lady said that "The president wants to know about one of your recipients, a young child in the Camden, New Jersey, district."

I asked, "The president of what?"

She answered, "The president of the United States—Ronald Reagan."

I replied that I was leaving at once for Camden to review the child's file and would call the president's office to reply in full.

Some of the secretaries asked me one day, "Do you like your work?" I answered that I considered myself the "luckiest of all men" because I was able to use public largesse to help hundreds and thousands of "poor souls."

And so days became weeks and they in turn became months and years. I had been caring for my mother for seventeen years since my father's death. After a fractured hip she became increasingly immobile and Alzheimer's disease began insidiously.

On September 1, 1983, I retired from the employ of the state of New Jersey.

9
Caretaker (September 1983–1990)

During the eighties, my mother and I enjoyed vacations each year in countries of Europe that we had not seen. One year we took my mother's oldest sister, Mary Feser, age eighty-seven, to the Fatima shrine in Portugal. We saw many acts of awe-inspiring faith. On that trip, we visited Madrid, Segovia, Toledo, Avila, and "the Jewel of the Mediterranean"—Barcelona. The elderly sisters enjoyed the trip and held up well.

In the fall of 1983, my mother, age seventy-eight, and I took my niece, Andrea Curran, age seventeen, for a visit to Greece and the Greek Islands of Crete, Mikonos, Rhodes, and Santorini. Andrea won two "jackpots" while aboard the Greek ship circling the Aegean. She bought a new dress and had her hair done with her winnings. While abroad, she decided not to go swimming in the pool because some European couples didn't bother to wear bathing suits. The trip was Andrea's graduation present, and she enjoyed it very much.

In the summer of 1985, my mother and I traveled across the United States in the company of my sister Kathleen, her husband, Ward Curran, and their daughters, Colleen and Andrea. Ward and I had rented a large Crown Victoria Ford station wagon for the trip.

We visited Aspen, Colorado, because it was my mother's birthplace. Our group enjoyed stops at Mesa Verde—the site of the Cliff Dweller Indians and Grand Canyon.

Many of our relatives resided in Southern California, and we visited cousin Mary-Louise Van Noy in Glendora and cousin Edith Cochran in Claremont.

We took the northern route through Wyoming, Denver, and Springfield, Illinois, where we visited Nathaniel Curran, Ward's father, age eighty at that time. When he saw me, he said, "Doctor, you're getting portly."

I replied, "Mr. Curran, your hearing seems to be down, but your eyesight is good."

My niece Colleen, age fifteen, wanted to see the Grand Ole Opry in Tennessee, so we headed for Nashville. We saw Roy Acuff,

Hank Snow, Reba McIntyre, and Minnie Pearl, all of whom were in the show.

When we returned the leased station wagon to Winner Ford in Haddonfield, we acknowledged that we had traveled 8,500 miles in three weeks.

My mother and I returned to our apartment on the first floor of my Victorian home in Haddonfield. The house, at 109 Kings Highway, contained twenty rooms and five full bathrooms. There were three other apartments besides our own. Although I had installed a new heating system and modernized all the bathrooms in 1965, I spent a good deal of my time maintaining the home and the premises.

My daily routine usually began by taking my mother to Our Lady of Grace Roman Catholic Church in Somerdale for 8:00 A.M. mass.

Following mass each day I performed many tasks at 109. The Romanesque Victorian home was built between 1873 and 1876. There were thirteen large columns around a large porch that surrounded most of the first floor. The eaves of the three-story building were sixty feet above ground level, and atop the structure was a good-sized "captain's walk," twelve feet square and about ten feet in height. The house was white and shutters dark green in color. The Haddonfield Historical Society included 109 in its list of historic buildings. I worked each day until noon—either painting, mowing the spacious lawn, planting flowers, or recoating the extensive driveway or parking area.

After lunch, my lifetime habit was an afternoon nap. Following our evening meal, I took my mother for a ride in the countryside.

Three elderly widows who were Social Security recipients occupied the three apartments other than ours. They also had garage facilities for their cars. I charged very modest rental fees. My mother liked them.

My mother took comfort in the fact that we could lock the doors each night at 9:00 P.M. There were no late-night or raucous parties.

As with most old houses, there were numerous "ghost stories." Locked doors suddenly opened; footsteps were heard on the stairs when no person was climbing them. There were strange noises in the night and even reports of apparitions, but my father always said, "Don't worry about the dead ones; it's the live ones who can cause concern."

Sometime in early 1988, my mother's oldest brother, William J. Loughman, age ninety-one at the time, phoned me to say that he had no place to live and because of age couldn't care for himself. Since he lived in California, my cousin William Feser arranged to fly with him to the Philadelphia International Airport. My brother Albert and I met them and brought them to Haddonfield. Uncle Bill was a fine old gentleman and had served thirty years in the U.S. Navy. He retired as a commissioned warrant officer. Now he was non-ambulatory and legally blind. I provided him with a bedroom close to a bathroom and kitchen, and he used a wheelchair.

Cousin William Feser returned to the West Coast after a three-day visit. Uncle Bill lived thirteen months with us and died peacefully in his sleep on an evening in June of 1989, about six months short of his ninety-third birthday.

During the last days of his life, he enjoyed reminiscing about his birthplace and childhood in Aspen, Colorado. He had joined the

U.S. Navy on St. Patrick's Day, 1913, and was assigned to the USS *Yankton*—the last sailing ship of the fleet. During World War II, he served on the destroyer USS *Cassin B. Young*. I think he thoroughly enjoyed the last year of his life with his sister and close family.

In late 1988 and during 1989, I met and courted Teresa R. Siniscalco, an English teacher in the Cherry Hill, New Jersey, school system. During this period, I made two momentous decisions for myself. The first decision was to sell 109 after nearly twenty-five years of ownership. The second decision was to marry the person who had won my heart.

Also, during this time, my mother showed increasing symptoms of Alzheimer's disease and no longer recognized me as her son.

10

Marriage and Family

On Saturday morning, June 30, 1990, at 11:00 A.M., Teresa Siniscalco and I were married. Monsignor Thomas Cannon, the pastor of Our Lady of Grace Roman Catholic Church of Stratford, New Jersey, officiated. My sister Margaret and her husband were our only attendants. The day was sunny and breezy, and the temperature was seventy-eight degrees Fahrenheit. After the ceremony, the four of us enjoyed a seafood dinner at a restaurant called Seafood Shanty. Teresa and I had a brief honeymoon visit to Princeton, New Jersey; we stayed at the Palmer House. We took up residence at 630 West Marlton Pike, Cherry Hill. It was Teresa's family residence. The house is a one-story stone structure with three bedrooms and two and one-half bathrooms. Teresa's sister, Marie, occupied one bedroom. My mother, age eighty-five, and Teresa's Aunt Mary occupied a second bedroom. Teresa and I occupied the master bedroom. The elderly ladies ultimately took up residence in the Stratford Nursing Home, located on Locust Road, Stratford, New Jersey. I knew the owners, the manager, and the attending physician, Dr. Warden. Teresa and I rejoiced in the knowledge that her aunt and my mother were well cared for.

In the spring of 1991, Teresa and I joined my sister Kathleen and her husband, Dr. Ward S. Curran, on a visit to England and Scotland. When we arrived at Heathrow Airport, London, we hired a Ford Explorer van. We traveled to the University of Essex and picked up my niece Colleen, who was a student there. The tour we planned was three weeks in length. It included visits to Cambridge University, York, Edinburgh, Loch Ness, and the Isle of Skye. We visited the train exhibit in Glasgow; at Stratford-on-Avon we enjoyed a play, *Henry IV,* by Shakespeare. We enjoyed a stay at Bath and admired the engineering skill of the ancient Romans. The last week of our tour was spent in London; visits to museums, castles, cathedrals, and theaters pleased everyone.

In the fall of 1992, Teresa's Aunt Mary

Author's home in Cherry Hill, NJ.

Author and wife, Teresa R. Jannett, aboard the ship *Cocktail Hour* in Summer 2001.

passed away in her sleep. My mother died in March of 1993. Fortunately, neither of them suffered in their last days.

In 1993, I underwent a trans-urethral resection of a benign enlargement of the prostate gland. Recovery was swift and results excellent.

From time to time, Teresa and I visited my sister Kathleen and her husband, Ward Curran, in Hartford, Connecticut. Likewise, we visited my sister Margaret and her husband, Joseph Goodyear, in Newark, Delaware. My brother, Albert, and two of his daughters had homes in Folsom, New Jersey—twenty-five miles distance from Cherry Hill. Because of the proximity we usually visited these families on a weekly basis on Saturday mornings.

Albert, my brother, was born on December 11, 1931, and weighed eight pounds upon delivery at the Esposito Home. As a child he had curly blond hair. Although, I was eight years older, I enjoyed playing with him. Al attended St. Joseph's Grammar School in Hammonton and then Malvern Prep in Malvern, Pennsylvania. He excelled in football and was All-State left halfback and at graduation took the award in chemistry. He served in the U.S. Army and witnessed the first hydrogen bomb explosion at Einewetok Island in the Pacific. While a student at Notre Dame University, he married Patricia Flaherty of Medford Lakes, New Jersey. Later he was awarded a degree in business administration. Albert and Patricia had four children, Mimi in 1956, Albert III in 1959, Patti in 1960, and Kim in 1966. Albert Junior worked with my father until his death in February 1966. They were homebuilders. My brother and later his son, Albert III, were employed by the U.S. Government, Department of the Navy, at Aviation Supply in Philadelphia, Pennsylvania. My brother built a lovely home in Folsom, New Jersey, in 1992, next to the two homes he built for his daughters and enjoys retirement there.

My sister Margaret was born on a rainy morning, April 4, 1927. She weighed seven and one-half pounds upon delivery at the Esposito Home in Hammonton. Margaret attended St. Joseph's Grammar School and Hammonton High School. During her childhood, she excelled in all forms of dancing—especially tap dancing and acrobatics. We called my sister Peggy. She was a good student and was accepted at Syracuse University in New York State, where she studied speech pathology and therapy. She was awarded a degree in 1948. Following her college studies, she worked in New York City as a buyer of costume jewelry for Kresge's department stores. She also did modeling for Jane Irwin Junior Miss Dress Company. In May of 1951, she married one of her classmates from Syracuse. Joe Goodyear was in one of Peggy's English classes at college. His major was journalism, and he worked for an advertising company—where he became executive vice president. Peggy and Joe had three children—Mark Elliott born in 1954, Brian born in 1958, and Margaret Elizabeth, who arrived in 1965. Joseph Goodyear was very successful in his work advertising a number of blockbuster drugs, including Miltown—an early tranquilizer. When he promoted sustained-release medication, he employed the noted artist Salvador Dali to prepare an exhibition at the AMA convention in Atlantic City. Peg and Joe retired to a home in Litchfield, Connecticut, in 1972. Thereafter he did freelance writing and completed a historical work on Sicily. During World War II, Joe was a navigator on a B-17 bomber out of England. On his twenty-fifth mission, his plane was shot down over Germany, and he spent a year as a POW. He was poorly fed at that time, and his weight decreased to ninety-five pounds. He was freed by the Soviet army in 1945. His health was never robust and he died of prostate cancer in 1996. Peggy was successfully treated for breast cancer several years ago and lives in her retirement home in Newark, Delaware.

My youngest sister, Kathleen (Kathy), was born on a very hot afternoon, July 8, 1937. I remember the day well. As a thirteen-year-old boy, I worked as a blueberry picker some seven miles from home on Weymouth Road. At two in the afternoon, we were sent from the fields as the temperature exceeded 100 degrees. That afternoon, I returned home on my bicycle. In the evening, I purchased a ninety-five-cent box of Whitman chocolates and visited my mother and new sister at the Esposito Home on Twelfth Street in Hammonton. My mother scolded me mildly for "wasting" money on candy. Kathy attended St. Joseph's Grammar School and High

School in Hammonton. She was a good student and enjoyed dancing school, where she excelled in toe dancing. Kathy attended Immaculata College in Washington, D.C., and then the Tobe-Coburn School of Fashion Design, residing at the Barbizon Hotel. Following, her schooling, Kathy worked as a representative for the National Cotton Council. The council consisted of 232 concerns engaged in the production of cotton and cotton manufacture. Her main office was in the Empire State Building in New York City. In 1963 Kathy met Dr. Ward Curran, and in November of that year they were married. On their honeymoon they enjoyed visits to Rome, Paris, and London. Ward had received his Ph.D. from Columbia University, where he majored in economics. During his career, he wrote many articles and three textbooks relating to his specialty. Kathy and Ward had two daughters: Andrea, born in 1965, and Colleen, born in 1970. After the two children completed their schooling and married, the parents settled in their comfortable home in West Hartford, Connecticut. After suffering a hip fracture, Ward continued his work as economics professor at Trinity College in Hartford but on a reduced schedule.

11
European Ancestry

Maternal Ancestry

My mother's parents were born and raised in Ireland. Her father was Michael Loughman (pronounced "*luke*-mon," with the accent on the first syllable). He was raised on a 177-acre dairy farm in the Golden Valley of county Cork. The family residence was a two-story Georgian-style home situated on a hill. He was the eldest son of William Loughman, known in the area as William "Tell" for his habit of telling people off, including the village priest.

My grandfather Michael was the oldest son and had the misfortune of racing his father's favorite horse to death. The mother of my grandfather, fearing her husband's violent temper and for the safety of her son, gave him money to go to America. He settled in Aspen, Colorado, in 1892. He was about twenty years old at the time. He was six feet tall, with flaming red hair. His nickname in Aspen was Red Mike. He was "high-strung," and when upset he stuttered.

In the 1890s, Aspen, Colorado, was a booming silver-mining town. One nugget of ore weighed 1,800 pounds and was almost pure silver. Upon arrival in Aspen, my grandfather worked in the mines. In 1893, my grandfather met and married a young Irish immigrant girl, Julia Harrington. She was from Eyries, Ireland, in county Clare. It was a town in southwestern Ireland where the mountains met the ocean.

Julia Harrington was a pretty Irish girl of medium height. She had curly chestnut brown hair and blue eyes. Her facial features were fine and her body thin. She had four brothers and a sister living in Aspen: John, Patrick, Michael, Jerome, and Mary.

My grandmother Julia had her first child, Mary, on October 27, 1894. The baby was well-formed, with auburn red hair, and destined to live to 102. Julia had five further pregnancies. William Loughman was Julia's first son, born February 13, 1896. Grandmother always called him her Valentine. Bernard

Loughman was born on May 15, 1900. He was destined to become a well-known lawyer in Ventura, California. As a child, he was very bright and scholarly and skipped two grades at a time in grammar school. Lawrence Loughman was born in November 1902. He had curly blond hair and a very outgoing friendly disposition. He was very bright. Later, as a young man, he earned an engineering degree from Drexel University and a law degree from the University of Colorado. He, too, settled eventually in Ventura, California, where he practiced law. My mother and her twin brother arrived on July 10, 1905. They were named Margaret and Florian. My mother had four children, two boys and two girls. Florian married Rose Murphy in Philadelphia, Pennsylvania, in 1930. He and his wife had five sons and two daughters. The last child of Michael and Julia was Louise—born in 1908.

During the 1890s, my grandfather Michael left the mines and started a "bottling works" for whiskey. He also had the franchise for Coors beer on the eastern slope of the Rockies. There were forty saloons in Aspen that Grandfather supplied with his products.

He was a teetotaler and, although he carried cigars for his customers, never smoked. For a decade or more "Red Mike's" business flourished. But his luck changed for the worse when his wife came down with tuberculosis. Then the mines filled with water and Aspen became a ghost town. The Loughman family traveled east to Newark, New Jersey, to consult with a relative—Dr. DeLaney. My grandmother was placed in a sanitarium—where she died of her disease in 1915 at the age of forty-two. The children, my mother included, were placed in an orphanage operated by an order of German nuns. The children of Michael and Julia remained in the orphanage in Newark until they were about fifteen years of age. My grandfather went to Butte, Montana, and assisted his brother who was ill.

Paternal Ancestry

My father's parents were born and raised in Gildone, Italy, a suburb of Compobasso in the Abruzzi-Molise Province. Five generations ago, Caesare Giovannitti was born and raised in Florence, Italy. He lived for a time in Torino and then settled in Campobasso. My grandfather was a fourth-generation grandson of Caesare named Fiorangelo Giovannitti. He was born in 1872 and immigrated to the United States at age nineteen in 1891. Upon arrival in America, he lived in Cleveland, Ohio, where he had relatives. In appearance, he was of medium height with light brown hair and hazel eyes. He was a skilled masonry craftsman and enjoyed playing the tuba in Italian bands.

In 1893, he met and married a pretty little Italian girl who had curly brown hair and big brown eyes. Her name was Emilia DiBiasio. She had known my grandfather in Italy when they were children. Her family were bakers and she and three of her sisters delivered bread in baskets to the customers in Gildone, Italy. My paternal grandparents moved to Germantown, Pennsylvania, where my grandmother had relatives. My grandfather started a masonry contracting business and leased quarries to furnish the stone needed for his work. My grandmother started an Italian specialty store near Chew and Chelton Avenues in Germantown. She sold fruit, vegetables, groceries, and meat. In addition to running her store and having children, she boarded young Italian men who worked in the quarries.

Between 1894 and 1912, my grandmother had ten children—eight sons and two daughters. The first child was Anna, born in May 1894, and the last child was Arthur, born July 4, 1912. There were few Italian families in Germantown in the 1890s. For business purposes Grandfather changed his name to Andrew F. Jannett. For health reasons my grandfather moved his family to Hammonton, located in the south central part of the state. The year was 1907. They had two horses and two wagons to move themselves, seven children, and their worldly possessions. Their youngest child was only two years old. They had to travel from Germantown to ferries crossing the Delaware River. Then they traveled thirty miles on gravel roads to Hammonton, a small town in the wilderness. The trip must have seemed interminable.

They lived at first on North Third Street, and their neighbors were Rocco Ruberton and his large family of five sons and three daughters. The town of Hammonton was truly a garden spot. Fruits, vegetables, and berries of every type were grown there. Most of the big farmers in those early years were not Italian. The few Italian families called them the Americans, or *Americanos.* But increasing numbers of Italian immigrants came to the South Jersey area starting in the 1880s. The Capellis, Rizzottes, and Campanellas became big growers. With the influx of more and more Italian immigrants, my grandfather's building business blossomed. Most of the immigrants came from Sicily (especially Gesso) and southern Italy. Skinner's Glass Factory and Galigne Shoe Company provided employment.

In 1913, my grandfather purchased a well-built brick home on the corner of Twelfth Street and Madison Avenue to accommodate his large family. Meanwhile, he established the Hammonton Lime and Cement Company at 24 Front Street opposite the Pennsylvania Railroad Station in Hammonton. He manufactured building blocks, bricks, and concrete products of all kinds. Being an enterprising man, he also entered the house raising and moving business. Like many Europeans, my paternal grandparents thought the ultimate good was the ownership of property. Between 1907 and 1927, they brought residential and commercial properties. In 1927, my grandmother Emilia became ill with liver cancer and passed away in the fall. My grandfather was devastated by the loss of his wife. He asked my father and mother to move into his large home to manage it and help care for his two teenage boys still living at home. My Uncle Andrew was seventeen and in high school. The younger brother, Arthur, was fifteen.

In the following year, 1928, my grandfather married Cecilia Coast, a forty-three-year-old schoolteacher. She was fifteen years younger than Grandfather. My parents, my sister Peggy, and I moved into our own house on South Egg Harbor Road. Within a year, Cecilia was pregnant. She developed eclampsia and delivery of a baby boy relieved the illness. The child, Ralph, had Down's syndrome or severe mental retardation and needed around-the-clock care. My two young uncles moved out of the big house into my Aunt Anna's home. A second pregnancy led to Cecilia's death. She refused to have an abortion to relieve eclampsia. She was a devoted Catholic and had played the organ in her church for many years prior to her marriage to my grandfather.

The stock market crash of 1929 led to the severe Depression of the 1930s. Home building and the need for building materials came to a halt. My grandfather would not institutionalize Ralph and employed nurses at home for him. By 1934, the child had died, but my grandfather had lost most of his property. He developed high blood pressure and died of a stroke in the fall of 1941. He was a man of good character and was revered by all of the family. He was affectionately called the Old Gent.

12
The First Three Generations in America

When I was fifteen years old in the summer of 1939, I went to visit New York City. During my two-week visit, I went to see the Statue of Liberty. I was impressed by the words inscribed on the monument base. They bear repeating here:

Give me your tired, your poor,
Your huddled masses yearning to breathe free,
The wretched refuse of your teeming shore,
Send these, the homeless, tempest-tossed to me:
I lift my lamp beside the golden door.

Like many immigrants before and after them, my grandparents on both sides yearned for a better life for themselves and their progeny. The first generation on both sides totaled seventeen persons. Only two of them attended college and graduate school. A few others attended high school. Most of them completed eighth grade. My father and his sister Anna only completed the fourth grade. They were put to work in Dobbins Cotton Mills at the tender ages of nine and eleven years, respectively. Their hours started early in the morning and continued to late afternoon. They placed cotton dollies on the machines. The few dollars per week that they earned were used to help support the growing family. The dream of education and the need of it to succeed in America was firmly fixed in their minds. Accordingly, the second and third generations on both sides totaled fewer then 100 persons. Of this group, there were two Ph.D.'s, two board-certified surgeons, three LL.D.'s (lawyers), four Ph.D.'s (pharmacists), two master degrees, and nearly twenty bachelor degrees. The schools that they attended included the most prestigious in the nation and numbered more than twenty colleges and universities such as Harvard, Johns Hopkins, the University of Pennsylvania, Notre Dame, Manhattanville, St. Leo's University, Colgate University, Syracuse, the University of Delaware, Trinity College in Hartford, and other well-known schools. In addition to academic achievements there were at least twenty persons who gained proficiency on various musical instruments. Ten persons played the piano well. A few excelled with the violin, trumpet, organ, flute, or guitar. On the military front, members of our families answered the call to duty in every war and took part in combat to protect our country and cherished freedoms. My father, Albert Michael, volunteered to serve in France as an ambulance driver at Verdun and Chateau-Thierry. He arrived in France before the American Expeditionary Force. Thus he was assigned to the French Sixty-eighth Blue Devils Division. Henry Ford supplied the ambulances that were driven by their USAACS (United States of America Ambulance Corps) at a one-dollar profit or above cost. The machines arrived in crates, and the American corpsmen were trained to assemble and maintain them. The military operations at the time required driving the Model T Ford ambulances in the Vosges Mountains in winter weather. My father's group carried more than 14,000 wounded to the aid stations and hospitals. The Amiens Cathedral, eighty-five miles north of Paris, was converted for a time to a hospital. At the war's end, General Petain pinned the Croix de Guerre medal on my father's uniform.

Three of my mother's brothers served in the U.S. Navy during World War I. Ens. Bernard Loughman and CPO William J. Loughman operated submarine chaser vessels out of Cape May Naval Station at Cape May, New Jersey. Their brother Lawrence served as an ordinary seaman. During a storm, a torpedo fell from its rack and Larry suffered a broken back. Initially, he was reported in newspapers as having been killed. But he survived and spent one year on his back in the U.S. Naval Hospital at San Diego, California. He walked with a decided limp for the rest of his life.

Upon the outbreak of World War II, my uncle Bill Loughman was called back to duty in the U.S. Navy. He had already served from 1913 until 1933 in the navy. At first, he served as a training officer ashore and later as chief quartermaster aboard the destroyer *Cassin B. Young*. Two of my father's younger brothers volunteered for duty in the U.S. Army during World War II. Anthony served in the Medics and Andy in Transportation. My cousin Donald Feser and I served in the U.S. Navy during World War II. Donald graduated from Columbia University Midshipman School as an ensign and was wounded in the invasion of Iwo Jima. I graduated from Notre Dame University Midshipman School with the rank of ensign and served on a Landing Craft Infantry (1075). Our group took part in the invasion of Mindoro, Luzon, and Mindanao in the Philippine Islands. We also took part in the invasion of Brunei in British Northwest Borneo.

My brother, Albert, served in the U.S. Army during the early 1950s in the Korean police action. He witnessed the explosion of the first hydrogen bomb at Einewetok Island in the Pacific.

During the Vietnam War, a cousin, John Feser, lost his right arm and left leg in battle. He died prematurely at age forty-five. He was a very brave man.

Epilogue

I came into the world about twenty years after the Wright brothers flew the first plane. It was about four years before Charles Lindbergh crossed the Atlantic Ocean in his *Spirit of St. Louis* single-engine plane. The home in which I grew up had an icebox to keep out perishables cold. A "pipeless" heater that burned chestnut-sized coal provided heat in the winter. Water for Saturday night baths was heated on a kitchen stove. Music was provided by a Victrola that was hand-cranked and needed new needles quite often. Later we got our first Atwater Kent radio. It needed a few minutes to warm up. If there was no static, we could get Station WJZ in New York or WOR in Newark. Occasionally a neighbor would brag that he got Cincinnati, Ohio.

My mother had a schedule. Mondays were clothes-washing days, Tuesday was ironing day, Wednesday and Thursday could be used for sewing on the Singer sewing machine and mending socks, Friday was house-cleaning day, and Saturday was used to polish the furniture. Sunday was church day and usually roasted chicken day.

Other than an occasional bout of measles, mumps, or chicken pox, we were seldom ill. When we did feel sick, Mother had all sorts of home remedies. Chicken soup and castor oil were high on her list. For sore throats, there was hot lemonade with honey. Earaches seemed to respond to sweet spirits of nitre applied behind the ears, and always a rubdown of Vicks for chest colds. If all of her nostrums failed, we called our beloved Dr. "Spotty" on our party line. A visit to the office cost fifty cents and a rare house call cost one dollar.

Medicine took a giant step forward during the 1930s with the introduction of sulfa drugs for control of infections. They were bacteriostatics. In the 1940s, penicillin was the "miracle drug." It was the first of the bactericidal drugs. Streptomycin, aureomycin, tetracyclines, erythromycin, and a host of others followed. As bacteria gained resistance, a search for new medicines was needed. The discovery of insulin in the 1920s revolutionized the way diabetes was treated. In the surgical field, many new procedures were devised. Early in the twentieth century, 85 percent of abdominal surgeries were termed exploratory laparotomies. By 1950, that figure was reduced to 15 percent. New diagnostic radiology techniques increased all physicians' acumen. All body cavities became accessible to the surgeon. In 1912, Dr. Harvey Cushing performed a removal of a brain tumor on Gen. Leonard Wood. In the 1930s, Dr. Evart Graham removed a lung tumor on a patient in Saint Louis. The chest cavity was entered and the patient had long-term survival. In 1939, Dr. Alfred Blalock of the Johns Hopkins Hospital performed blue baby operations. In the late 1940s and 1950s, Dr. Charles Bailey of Hahnemann Hospital in Philadelphia performed hundreds of heart operations and brought the mortality rate for mitral commissurotomies to under 5 percent. At about the same time, Dr. John Gibbon, professor of surgery at Jefferson, invented the first heart/lung machine, facilitating transplantation of organs. The next triumph will be the cure of cancer. In 1993, Novartis A.G. developed a drug designed to block the protein that causes leukemia in mice. In 1998, the oral medication gleevec was first tested on people and found to be more than 90 percent effective in a trial with 532 people. About eight thousand leukemia patients now receive gleevec. Side effects of the drug have been minimal. The new paradigm of cancer therapy will now be used against a whole panoply of cancers. The FDA of the United States was the first agency to approve gleevec for human beings. All the world's peoples hope and pray that they will be relieved of cancer's scourge.

GEORGE W. BUSH

****************AUTO**3-DIGIT 080
Dr. Andrew F. Jannett
630 Marlton Pike W
Cherry Hill, NJ 08002-3506

January 16, 2001

Dear Dr. Jannett,

Dick Cheney and I want to thank you for all you have done for us. Your leadership, energy, and generous commitment of time were crucial to our campaign's success.

I am grateful for your hard work and honored you were on my team. I look forward to leading our great country.

Sincerely,

George W. Bush

PAID FOR BY REPUBLICAN NATIONAL COMMITTEE. AUTHORIZED BY BUSH/CHENEY 2000, INC.
NOT PAID FOR AT TAXPAYERS EXPENSE.